A Practitioner's Study – Volume 2

Insights Into Confined Space Rescue

Pat Rhodes

Disclaimer

This book is intended for use by confined space rescue technicians who are trained and certified in the applied disciplines of confined space rescue. Confined space rescue demands attention to every detail. Even if the techniques, procedures and illustrations in this book are diligently followed, serious injury and/or death may result. This book makes no claim to be all-inclusive on the subjects of confined space rescue. The opinions set forth within this document are strictly those of the author.

There is no substitute for quality training under the guidance of qualified, expert confined space rescue instructors.

Insofar as the author of this book has no control over the level of expertise of the reader of this material, or the manner this information is used, the author assumes no responsibility for the reader's use of this book.

There is no warranty, either expressed or implied, for the accuracy and/or reliability for the information contained hereof.

A Practitioner's Study Volume 2: Insights Into Confined Space Rescue, © Copyright 2018, Rhodes. All rights reserved for the contents of this book. NO unauthorized duplication by any means without prior written permission from the author.

A Practitioner's Study – Volume 2:
Insights Into Confined Space Rescue

*Confined Space Rescue Rigging Considerations for
Industry, Construction and Fire/Rescue*

Pat Rhodes

Haec stercore periculosum est. Custodite animas vestras.

Contents

Introduction 4
A Brief History of Gratitude 5
Ode to Abraham Maslow 8
Confined Space and Standby-Rescue is a Trade 11
Professional Confined Space Rescue Teams 16
The Confined Space Environment 18
A.I.R. 25
(Assessment, Isolation, Resources), the role of Incident Management during a confined space emergency 25
    Assessment 26
        What happened? 26
        What are the hazards? 27
        Victim Profile 27
    Isolation 28
        Control access to the area. 28
        Hot, Warm, and Cold Zones 28
        Lockout, Tagout 31
        Atmospheric Monitoring 33
    Resources 37
        Ventilation 38
        Personal Protective Equipment 41
Confined Space Extrication and Rigging 44
    Confined Space Rigging Equipment Considerations 44
    Knotty Thoughts for Confined Space Rescue 54
    Rescue Anchorage Considerations for Industry 71
    Belay Concepts Applied in an Industrial Fall Arrest World 81
    The Integration of the Mainline with Standards Compliancy 86
    Personal Vertical Mobility 96
    Towers and Vertical Confined Space Structures 101
    Highline Rigging Suggestions 103
Appendix 1: Applied Rigging Physics 106
Appendix 2: Elevated Anchor Systems 115
End Notes: 117

Introduction

There are numerous high quality training manuals on the market today that address the typical OSHA driven requirements for confined space rescue. It was never my intent to write an additional one. This book is simply my sharing of perceptions on a few confined space considerations that I have personally encountered during my career of rescue work in and around the confined space environment.

It should also be noted that this book is an extension of my previous book *A Practitioner's Study About Rope Rescue Rigging*. I have included some direct rigging information from the *Practitioner's Study About Rope Rescue Rigging*, and in a few instances, such as the sections addressing knot craft and highlines, I have added changes and/or improvements to the rigging practices that are directly taken from the *Practitioner's Study*.

To paraphrase Reed Thorne, many issues in the rescue profession may be categorized as being either peripheral or central. Peripheral issues are those that allow for some choices on the methodology of getting something accomplished, whereas central issues are non-negotiable. When first learning a subject, we are categorically presented with very specific techniques to reach an end result, in essence, everything seems to be non-negotiable central issues. We are told how to do something, and don't deviate from what you are told. As we become more savvy to specific techniques and goals, we naturally gain more freedom in our skill sets and we start to ask about the reasoning behind the instruction. In other words, what is the *why* behind the *how*? Today, at least in the way I personally think about rigging, my universal central issues are; gravity, friction, compression and tension, torque and bending moment. My prime central belief in the confined space realm is*; never become complacent*. Confined space work must be researched, calculated and absolutely accountable. Ultimately, I would say my most important central foundation in this world of rescue is...study and practice daily, as much as possible, ongoing and never ending.

These considerations are the driving force behind this book. It would be foolhardy for me to attempt a publication that claims to have all the answers for confined space rescue. However, I can share with you some of my personal experiences, favorite knots and evolving rigging concepts in hopes that you may find some bit of information that you can use and possibly add to your bag-of-tricks.

A Brief History of Gratitude

An Acknowledgment of some of my greatest Influences in Rescue

As I reflect back on my life in technical rescue I can identify at least seven events that were major catalysis in my career: My career in rescue officially started on March 7, 1977. That was my first day at the Phoenix Fire Department Academy as a new firefighter recruit. It was shortly after that I had my first rope rescue class. We were shown how to make a body harness (out of some old Gold Line rope) and how to pull someone out of a trench. I will always be grateful for my 28 years with Phoenix Fire, the education and experience they afforded me, and my lifelong Phoenix Fire Family. I can truly attest that the Phoenix Fire Department is one of the most progressive fire departments in the world.

By 1984 I had been assigned to "C" Shift as a firefighter, rescue/hazmat technician at Phoenix Fire Department's Station 4. On November 15, 1984, the day before my scheduled shift, Station 4 "B" shift responded to a confined space rescue involving a worker down in a predominately empty tank of toluene. During the process of working this emergency response, the tank exploded-killing my good friend Ricky Pearce. In addition, most of Station 4 "B" shift were sent to the hospital that day. As a result, I was called in from home to help finish the shift for my downed "B" Shift brethren. Later that same day, around sunset, those of us on the reserve truck went to the scene of the explosion. The memory of that sight haunts me to this day. It was the telling remains of a scene of complete chaos and panic. Those of us in the fire/rescue service always seem to think that we are under complete control while handling someone else's emergency…but that fragile control quickly abandons us when one of our own goes down. The one thing that stuck with me was that we often fail to realize the magnitude, both personal and social, of the results of our potentially misguided actions. Another important consideration is that we simply don't train adequately under the guidance of high-quality instructors.

It was at that point in my personal career, after the death of my good friend, that I realized that I was not training to my full potential. It was at that point that I made a career commitment to myself to raise the bar in my personal training. I have been obsessed with my own training ever since. I would grab onto any training in technical rescue I could get my hands on.

I was feeling pretty cocky about my rope rigging skills. During the spring of 1998, Phoenix Fire sent me to a tower/structural steel rope rescue course. The instructor of that class was this long-haired, mountain man looking fellow named Reed Thorne. It took very little time in the classroom on the first day for me to realize that this guy knew rigging better than anyone I had met, indeed, Reed's rigging was (and still is) an art form. After that first exposure to Reed's "Art of Clean Rigging" I was hooked on his methodology. I couldn't take enough Ropes That Rescue courses. It got to the point that Reed couldn't get rid of me, so he hired me on as an RTR instructor. My career with RTR lasted up to 2004 before I set out on my own to start my own rescue training company. Today when I reflect back on those days working under Reed Thorne's tutelage, I have to say with great pride and humility, that was my period of greatest growth in my career of rope rigging. To Reed Thorne, I am eternally grateful. To all the other rope access and rescue practitioners out there, go up the mountain and take a course from Reed Thorne at Ropes That Rescue…you will be enlightened!

Around the year of 2000, during my time instructing for RTR, I was privileged to have a group of firefighters from the state of Michigan come to one of the RTR Sedona, Arizona rope rescue classes. Keep in mind, these fellows chose to come to this seven-day class, across the country, and on their own dime. One of the key members of this Michigan contingency was David Van Holstyn (VH-1). I have always considered David to be a true subject matter expert in multiple fields of technical rescue. In addition to being a current lead instructor for Ropes That Rescue, David is still a major rescue influence in the State of Michigan, indeed, throughout the United States. To this day, VH-1 remains my close friend and trusted advisor.

In 2009 I was contracted as a rescue consultant and instructor for Cascade Steel Rolling Mills in McMinnville, Oregon to help them start up their own in-house rescue team. My first impression of Cascade Steel was that the steel industry was truly an extremely dangerous work environment. The diversity of man operated cranes, molten steel, and mountains of scrap metal would raise the hair on the back of any seasoned rescuer. For these hardened steel workers, this place is just another day on the job. What I personally take from Cascade Steel is the firm belief that anyone who works every day in such a place is truly a subject matter expert of that particular environment. What better individuals to have on a rescue team than the very people that understand the inner workings of their workplace? To this day, the team at Cascade Steel, under the leadership of Dan Fisher, and Kenn Lindsey have formed and maintained one of the most skilled rescue teams I have had the privilege to work with, private or public. Currently this team has expanded their influence into their community of McMinnville, Oregon. With the ongoing efforts of the McMinnville Fire Department combining their resources with the team at Cascade Steel we are now witnessing a prototype rescue program that has evolved to provide one of the most efficient rescue services of any community in the United States. The commitment of the management of a private company, the open-mindedness of a municipal fire service, and the doggedness of all the members on both sides of the equation to get out and train on a regular and frequent basis is extraordinary. This inspires me in my continual commit to the long-term goals of a rescue career and my personal efforts as an instructor.

In 2013 I had the good fortune of traveling to Australia to work, teach and study with some truly outstanding rope access and rescue practitioners. Most notably, Richard Delaney, Dal Atkenson, Robert Dunshea, William Proctor, and Rob Stringer. Even though I was brought in to instruct a rigging physics course for these heavy hitters enrolled in the class, the line between instructor and student became immediately blurred to me. I think I probably learned more from them than they did from me! Indeed, I would highly recommend any class offered by any of these world-class instructors. To all my Australian family, thank you for your years of support and friendship!

My career in rigging and rescue has brought me to where I am today. I am now the Safety and Rescue Compliance Manager for Kary Environmental Services (KES). Our home office is in Mesa, Arizona. KES is a well-established provider of hazardous material management. Not only does this company deal with the cleanup of nasty life-threatening conditions that pose environmental dangers to our communities, much of the time these highly skilled technicians are required to venture into what would seem to be impossible locations. This profession requires advanced rescue skills combined with detailed and well-orchestrated rescue plans. Additionally, KES provides standby-rescue for several industrial and construction clients that require advanced rescue support. My personal education in this fantastic world of safety and rescue is continuing to grow through daily collaboration with the dedicated team at KES.

Lastly, and most importantly, to my beloved Wife, Cheryl; it is fair to say that I would not be where I'm at today in my profession without your endless love, support and encouragement.

Ode to Abraham Maslow

My 40 plus years of rescue experience spreads out over a multiplicity of developmental stages of competence. The growth and evolution of any particular skill through the course of one's lifetime can be amazing and humbling. Regardless of their professions and passions, most people of my age can make similar career observations. I have often noted that rope and confined space rescue is a trade. Like all trades, the new apprentice must buy into the time commitment. A step by step commitment that stays humble throughout the pecking order of the journeyman gauntlet.

Of course, everyone learns at different speeds. Much of this is dependent on the depth of their passion for whatever it is they're trying to master. This is most evident in professions that deal in some aspect of preserving human life. Doctors must go through the better part of a decade of higher education before they typically reach a level of practitioner. Nurses must have several years of college. Paramedics, EMTs, Firefighters, and police officers must complete months, sometimes years of training and accreditation. Amazingly, this immense commitment of expensive education only get these dedicated guardians of human life over the starting line of their journeymen race. Once the journeymen ticket is punched, it takes several more years of applied work to gain true mastery. It requires a career commitment. In the end, no one ever stops learning.

Through my personal experiences with the fire/rescue service, I strongly feel that the same type of educational commitment must take place in order to achieve the level of a true practitioner of rescue. I have conducted countless rigging, rescue, rope access and confined space workshops, and seminars. Many of these courses were three, five, seven, nine, even 12 days in length. Some fire service rescue technician training programs I've been involved in lasted a full month. All these blitzkrieg type courses are categorically inadequate unless the participant uses them as a springboard to further their journey through a career choice. As much as I love this work – the truth is – technical rescue, and the necessity for rope access is, and always will be minimal when compared to the socioeconomic issues of today's global culture. There is only room for the serious. You should consider another career path if you are not truly committed to a lifelong study in professional rescue.

I've participated in issuing innumerable certificates for various course completions. At times I felt guilty about this certificate process that I have been an accomplice to. Worse yet, cooked training logbooks documenting "required time on rope" are often suspicious. Several course completion certificates and dubious rope access logbooks at times empower horribly undertrained, and misguided rescue and/or rope access apprentices in the belief that they can perform a very serious and dangerous function that involves some aspect of vertical manipulation of a human load. The great majority of certificates we often issue in the rescue world pale in comparison to the accountability of a diploma a health care graduate receives from an institution of higher learning. How do we raise the educational bar for rescue?

Levels of the Conscious Competence Learning Model[i]

I often paraphrase Abraham Maslow's conscience competence learning model as it applies the rescue profession. The allegorical play on the terms conscious and competent may be applied to any topic of learning. It also requires a large degree of humility and patience to walk this path on a daily basis. The truth is, in some aspect, *all of us* reside in all of the stages of consciousness and competent growth.

- ***Unconsciously Incompetent***

    Individuals who are unconsciously incompetent do not understand, or simply, don't even see their lack of knowledge of rescue related skills. To advance forward in this subject, these individuals must own their incompetence, and accept the value of these skills. Unfortunately, many of these unconsciously incompetent individuals are the ones at the management level who have been burdened with the responsibility to put together some sort of rescue component that almost always involves the purchasing of training and equipment. To sell a quality program to the unconsciously incompetent is usually a tall order. The unconsciously incompetent most often ask all the wrong decision-making questions: What solution is the least expensive? How can it be completed in the shortest amount of time? Of course – what kind of certificate are you going to issue? Last but not least…what kind of tee-shirt or ball cap are you giving us?

- ***Consciously Incompetent***

    Although these individuals do not understand what rescue is, they at least acknowledge their lack of skill and thus become open to the learning process. Here is where humility kicks in. It requires the individual to suck it up and admit that he or she doesn't have the answers, in fact, he or she probably doesn't even know what he or she is talking about. Only at this point of admission can the individual actively seek council in the next step in the right direction. This enlightenment in and of itself requires diligence in the selection of a high-quality training provider and subsequent research and selection of equipment.

- ***Consciously Competent***

    With time, patience, and practice, the individual now has some understanding of applied rigging physics and rescue in their environment. Nonetheless, performing the skills associated with these new skills typically demands degrees of deliberation. However, given time, the consciously competent individual can perform the needed skills and might be deemed skilled enough to graduate from the level of apprentice to journeyman.

- ***Unconsciously Competent***

    Individual journeymen who apply their many training courses over a period of many years and display a learning passion for rescue eventually become true practitioners of this trade. All aspects of rope rigging itself become instinctive and often committed to muscle-memory. Applied rigging physics is seen at all times. Very little in the world of rigging escapes this rescue wizard's eyes.

- ***Consciously Competent of Unconscious Competence***

    These few individuals reach such a high level of mastery of the subject of rescue that they are capable of consciously witnessing and fully understand and utilize the nature of those who are spread throughout the spectrum of the previous four stages of competence. These are the true subject matter experts and master instructors.

Confined Space and Standby-Rescue is a Trade

With all the focus I've already put on the need for a career commitment in rescue, how does this translate into a usable skill set for the everyday tradesman who are required to perform other jobs. I often refer to them as part-time rescuers, or incipient emergency responders. Applicable rescue knowledge does require a career commitment on the part of the employee and the employer alike. A career commitment to safety and rescue is arguably more important than the everyday primary job the employee was hired to do.

Even though this skill we call rescue requires a career commitment, it does come in many forms and styles that are customized to the everyday influences of any given work environment. The food processing company that might deal with grain silos and factory confined spaces has very different rescue profile from the maintenance crews who work every day on high voltage transmission towers, or the roughneck who works on an oil drilling platform 20 miles offshore, or the highrise window washer. Nonetheless, the food processor, the transmission lineman, the roughneck, the window washer, and their respective bosses must all make a career commitment to safety and the appropriate form of rescue. The complexities and training requirements will vary, however, the commitment to high quality and frequent training is non-negotiable.

Fire/Rescue Personnel vs. Industrial Rescue Personnel

As I have stated many times, my 28 years with the Phoenix Fire department was a developmental springboard for my career in technical rescue, and standby rescue work. However, if I may be brutally honest, it wasn't until the twilight of my fire service career when I started to understand the naivety of my fire service training and how little of it actually applied to the exceedingly complex real world of OSHA driven industrial/construction safety and rescue.

What are the pros and cons for staffing a confined space standby rescue team with off-duty fire/rescue personnel?

Due to the fact that most fire department response is medical, firefighters are typically extremely seasoned at delivering emergency medical services. However, this seasoned EMS background, although nice to have, is usually *not* credentialed when used outside the EMT's professional fire service employer. Consequently, a standby rescue contractor who uses off-duty firefighters might not be able to legally claim that they can provide EMS services simply based on the rescuer's EMS education.

To think that rope and confined space rescue trained firefighters make the best rescuers for a standby job is, at best, highly speculative. Fire/rescue response, by its very nature, is reactive. Most often, the 911 responder hits the road with little or no knowledge of the specifics of the emergency they are responding to. As such, OSHA law has historically turned a blind eye to typical OSHA violations that are abundant during an unplanned fire/rescue response.

> Example; typical fire/rescue belay line methodology, whether it be tandem prusiks, or the MPD, or any number of *human controlled* fire service belay systems, most often is not compliant with OSHA fall arrest criteria. Yet, the fire department gets away with it because of perceived social acceptance of their unplanned response. Providing no one gets injured or dies, OSHA will give the fire service a compliance mulligan every time!

Most often, the off-duty firefighters who hire on to perform a standby rescue job simply do not know any better; they typically have minimal training in OSHA compliancy. Like any good firefighter, they will default to the methodology their department instructors taught them. Why is this a big deal? Proactive standby-rescue is the polar opposite to the reactive/911 response. Standby-rescue must be intensely *proactive* in terms of jobsite preparation. Standby-rescues must be driven by detailed rescue plans that include blueprints of the rigging complete with approved anchor placements and math and physics calculations for critical rigging angles and anticipated worst case scenario loads. In fact, the standby-rescue must be so planned out that the probability of an actual rescue is close to zero percent.

This is not to dissuade the use of firefighters for industrial standby rescue. With appropriate study in OSHA standards and practice in quality industrial rope access skills, combined with highly detailed pre-plans; firefighters may become good standby-rescuers. Of course, this same litany of rescue skills, education and planning holds true with industry personnel who choose to get into standby-rescue work. The bottom line is, simply being a trained technical rescue firefighter does not necessarily qualify that individual for standby-rescue. Conversely, having subject matter expertise of a specific jobsite is a key factor for an industrial standby rescuer. However, being a jobsite subject matter expert with little (if any) dedicated rescue training doesn't qualify that person for standby-rescue either.

Jobs that Require Standby-Rescue

The trades of standby-rescue as well as rope access are, first and foremost, comprised of skills that may be used at numerous jobsites and locations. There are three basic realities that must be acknowledged:

1. Standby-rescue must be considered an option when any jobsite or public gathering poses a threat to health and safety of the occupants and/or participants within that location.

2. Standby-rescue must be designed for the specific work environment it is to be used in.

    No two trades, or, no two work environments are the same. Logic dictates that no singular, cookie cutter methodology will ever completely meet the needs of all work environments. Standby-rescue training is best served when driven by the subject-matter expertise of the employees that are actually doing the work. This is combined with high quality research and development and instruction that is based on sound rigging physics. If the rescue program doesn't meet the environmental needs of the worksite than the program must be changed.

3. A detailed rescue plan must be designed and a rescue system must be pre-rigged and in place prior to the start of any work. This should apply to rope access jobs as well as confined space work. Standby-rescue should be a highly strategic and prearranged event. Each aspect of the standby-rescue plan should be calculated and rehearsed. As such, all components of the rescue should be in place and pre-rigged for immediate activation. When possible, the rescue system should be controlled from the anchors in such a way that no worker should have to personally access the victim to complete the rescue. Conditions should be identified during the planning of the job if rescuers are required to make entry and/or go vertical. In this case, rescue personnel with advanced skills should be in place during the duration of the job.

And like all trades, any rescue discipline is a practiced skill that if done right, will take a career commitment to master. This is how the American workforce should view the practice of standby-rescue. Workers, by their very nature are willing to go the extra distance, especially when one of their co-workers is in trouble and in need of help. Why then not go the extra mile and learn how to rescue the safest and most expedient way possible?

Rescue is also the insurance policy of a good safety program

From the company's prospective, quality in-house rescue is the insurance policy of a good safety program. Like most insurance policies, we probably don't like the premiums, but we would never drive without auto insurance, and most of us have health insurance. In most States auto and health insurance is mandated by law. The consequences of not having a good insurance policy can become devastating and much more expensive in the long run. Yes, providing a viable rescue contingency is expensive and time consuming. Yes, employers hope they never have to use their rescue team. Yes, providing rescue at the work place that meets the hazard potential of the work environment is the law.

Prime Directive for Standby-Rescue

Above all else, our primary directive is the absolute safety of everyone involved in whatever rescue event that is underway. It is the one central belief that drives this book.

Safety is a complex word. The term safety is one of the most spoken in our industrial society, and yet, I would argue that it is a concept that is most abused, or at least, the most misunderstood. Safe practices in the workplace is abundant in countless publications and standards, and yet, every day we are presented with a new example of a serious injury or fatality due to lack of performance in a safe manner while at work. Written standards are needed; however, it is frequent safety and rescue training that promotes a heightened state of situational awareness of existing hazards within the work environment.

Rescue is a component of the safety program. It would serve employers to remember that in-house rescue team members should be agents of the safety program. With a total buy-in of this concept, the likelihood of a serious accident is greatly reduced. Preventing the need for a rescue is the best rescue of all!

Rope access is a critical component for standby-rescue.

Rope access skills is quickly becoming a critical requirement of any viable standby-rescue team. With an increase in the popularity of rope access worldwide an ongoing debate is brewing in the United States over the legality of rope access through the eyes of OSHA. Although the winds of change are blowing, there currently is no *Federal* OSHA standard that specifically addresses rope access. However, some state plans have already made the jump. Most notably Cal OSHA. Most believe it is a matter of time before Federal OSHA produces their interpretation.

CALOSHA §3270.1. It is important to note the Scope and Applications of this section:

§3270.1. Use of Rope Access Equipment.

"Rope supported work shall be permitted only when other means of access are not feasible or would increase the risk of injury to the employee and/or the public. The requirements of this section include, but are not limited to, the inspection of dams and spillways, access to interior or exterior structural and architectural component of buildings, highway/bridge inspections and maintenance, and access to power plant penstocks."

Engineered scaffolding has a long history as the best practice of work at height and fall protection in the United States. The use of scaffolding will not change anytime soon. The language of CALOSHA §3270.1 says as much. It makes no claim to change or replace the use of scaffolding. We do not have permission to choose rope access over scaffolding, unless one of those extremely remote environments presents itself where scaffolding is simply not a realistic option.

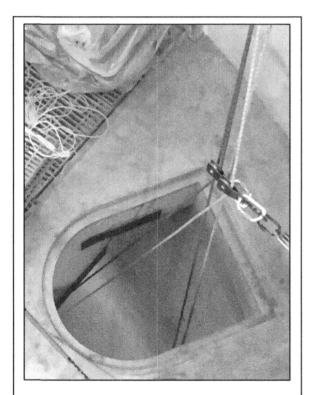

Engineered rope access systems being used for work on the walls of a 300' vertical shaft.

The fact is, Federal OSHA already allow work at height access for those situations where scaffolding is not possible. This is found in OSHA 1926.502(e) "Positioning device systems." The term "Positioning device systems" is arguably synonymous with rope access. Positioning systems must limit any fall to less than two feet. Positioning systems shall be secured to an anchorage capable of supporting at least twice the potential impact load of an employee's fall or 3,000 pounds (13.3kN), whichever is greater. The manufacturing design of most of today's rope access gear easily meet this criterion when used correctly.

It should also be noted that OSHA regulation, 1910.27(b), specifically addresses rope descent systems in general industry. In this standard, OSHA mandates that anchorage must be at least 5,000 pounds for each worker.

Professional Confined Space Rescue Teams

Preparation

As stated earlier, preparation for any confined space job is of the utmost importance. Rescue events are no different. What can be radically different in the rescue world is the amount of time that is available for pre-planning. In general, we can define three major divisions for professional rescue:

1. In-house industrial rescue teams
2. Standby rescue teams
3. Fire service and government response teams

In-house Industrial Rescue Teams

Professional in-house rescue teams are made up of company employees that were trained exclusively to provide onsite emergency response. Good examples would be full time fire brigades or full time emergency response teams. We would see this type of organization in large corporate factory/manufacturing locations. With the in-house team rescue preparation and pre-planning is mostly based on known factors and conditions that are typically present onsite any given day. As such, documented rescue pre-plans should always be readily available and well-practiced. These rescue plans should be simple in design, yet, very specific on identifying the following items of each rescue potential onsite:

1. Name and Location
2. Required rescue equipment needed
3. Required number of rescue personnel
4. Anchor identification and locations
5. A written outline and tactical drawing of the rescue

Standby rescue events must be highly planned. This planning and time allotment allow for complex setups such as this cantilever "A" Frame TerrAdaptor. The reactive lack-of-time nature of a 911 fire/rescue response would typically not allow enough time for such a setup.

In-house teams should be made aware of work taking place in high-profile rescue areas. By taking this proactive approach, such items as advanced rigging or time-consuming setups of Multipod configurations can be in place prior to the start of work. Save time on the setup so that the extrication process can be started as soon as possible.

Standby Rescue Teams

Standby rescue teams are professional top guns of rescue (or at least they should be). There are more and more charlatan companies popping up all the time. As a potential client wanting to hire a standby rescue team, it is vital to perform quality vetting. This should include resumes of each rescuer that is to be onsite, license and bonding of the rescue company and possibly a performance demonstration of their abilities in completing the rescue potential in a safe and timely manner.

Additionally, the standby rescue company should provide a written rescue plan that includes.
1. Name and Location
2. Required rescue equipment needed
3. Required number of rescue personnel
4. Anchor identification and locations
5. A written outline and tactical drawing of the rescue

Like in-house teams, advance knowledge of the rescue potential location and requirements combined with quality pre-rigging is a huge advantage for expediting the rescue event.

Fire Service and Government Response Teams

The fire service/municipal response may or may not be properly trained to perform a complex confined space rescue on any given day. The fire department is at a distinct disadvantage when responding to a technical rescue due to the lack of subject matter expertise of a given location. Fire departments do their best to stay on top of potential rescues in their area of response. However, each new day brings with it a completely different set of conditions and factors that must be addressed prior to the initiation of the actual rescue. As we have discussed earlier, the fire service operates in more of a reactionary mode versus the in-house teams or standby teams that are proactive on their setups and planning. As such, the fire service must perform in a more down and dirty manner simply due to the fact that they do not have the luxury of time that is required to rig more extravagant systems. Conversely, fire department rescue teams should be highly proficient in quick attack rope rigging techniques that promote vertical mobility using rope access skills.

The Confined Space Environment

Confined spaces account for multiple deaths and countless injuries every year. Many of these deaths are would-be rescuers, including fellow employees, by-standers, and emergency services members. Even with our strict OSHA regulations these unfortunate events continue. There is one culprit we can point our finger at the vast majority of times…complacency.

Confined spaces come in many forms, and they can be found throughout all phases of our society. A confined space is defined by OSHA as a space that is large enough to enter and perform work, has restricted means of access and egress, and is not designed for continuous occupancy.
A permit-required confined space is defined as a confined space that has at least one of the following hazardous conditions:
- Contains, or has the potential to contain an atmospheric hazard
- Contains material that has the potential for engulfment
- An internal configuration such that an entrant could become trapped
- Contains any other recognized serious safety or health hazards

Workers in confined spaces may be exposed to multiple hazards which may cause injury, illness, or death. Research from the National Institute for Occupational Safety and Health (NIOSH) tells us that oxygen-deficient, toxic and explosive atmospheres are the official leading cause of most reported fatalities and injuries in confined spaces. Whereas this statement is true, I often wonder if apathy, complacency, and ignorance should be included in this notorious list. After all, human beings made the decision to enter potentially oxygen-deficient atmospheres. Many times, sadly, workers simply don't know what they don't know. Hence, the value in NIOSH and OSHA, we must never lessen our efforts in educating the workforce on the hazards associated with confined spaces.

Hazards of Confined Spaces

My fundamental rule for anyone planning to enter a confined space is *Never become complacent.*

What may look like a harmless situation may be a potential threat. Hydrogen Sulfide can impair your ability to smell, giving a false sense of security that the hazard is no longer present. Additionally, some of the most lethal gases and vapors in existence have little or no odor at all!

The three most common atmospheric conditions that constitute hazards are:

Oxygen Deficiency

Normal fresh air contains 20.9% oxygen. OSHA states the any atmosphere containing less than 19.5% oxygen is considered to be oxygen deficient.

Oxygen deficiency may occur in areas where the level of oxygen has been reduced below 20.9. Although there are many causes, some common sources are; extreme rust in enclosed spaces, decomposition, and displacement from other gases. Inert gases such as nitrogen and carbon dioxide are commonly used in industry to purposely displace oxygen to eliminate potential combustion. Carbon dioxide is heavier than air and can easily form pockets at the bottom of confined areas. Carbon dioxide is commonly used in fire suppression systems in areas containing extra high voltage equipment such is seen in hydroelectric dams.

Combustible Gas and Vapors

Gas vapors are a concern due to the potential of and explosion when combined with the right mixture of an oxidizer and ignition.

Many ignitable vapors have a greater density than air making them extra problematic when they are free to sink to lower levels of a confined space such as sumps, and vessels. Due diligence is paramount in the atmospheric monitoring of all levels of a confined space. This is true not only for the monitoring of combustibles, but also for oxygen displacement vapors and toxic gases.

Toxic Gases or Vapors

Toxic gases and vapors will always be a permanent by-product of our industrial society. Even when storage tanks are empty for maintenance, small amounts of potential toxins will always hang around. Being exposed to the smallest parts per million of many types or residual toxic chemicals may be fatal in hours or even minutes. Typically the two most common toxic gases we want to monitor for are hydrogen sulfide (H_2S) and carbon monoxide (CO).

Carbon monoxide (CO) a product of incomplete combustion, is a common asphyxiant that has the propensity over oxygen to bond to our hemoglobin.

Hydrogen Sulfide (H2S) is usually a product of decomposition and is very common anywhere organic material can settle and proliferate the decaying process. Storm drains, and oil refineries are common breeding grounds for H2S. H_2S has a rotten egg odor. However, don't get caught in the trap thinking it's no longer around because you don't smell it anymore. H2S is notorious for desensitizing the olfactory nerve (our trigger for smelling).

Other Confined Space Hazards

Temperature Extremes:
Extremely hot or cold temperatures are magnified in confined spaces. The company I'm employed by, Kary Environmental Services, commonly cleans municipal water aquifers, during the summer months in Phoenix these locations are like working is a sauna. We will include cool vest for PPE, each employee is equipped with a drinking water-pack, and the ventilation is refrigerated. Additionally, crew are rotated on a regular basis.

Engulfment:
Engulfment hazards may be described as loose solids and/or liquids rapidly overcome a space with such speed that any people inside cannot escape. The first thing that might come to mind in thinking about engulfment is a predictable event in grain silos. This is indeed a notable cause of engulfment fatalities. However, there is many other examples of engulfment that may be much less predictable such as underground construction where infrastructure decay has allowed the buildup of large pockets of water on the exterior of the same tunnels that workers are inside of for repairs. Even more common, inadequately shored trenches have been the undoing of many workers. Are engulfment potentials predicable? Absolutely!

Noise:
Noise within a confined space will always be amplified because of design of the echo chamber you're inside of. Try to minimize excessive noise. When tools are being used hearing protection must be immediately available and easily accessible to every entrant. Headsets with radio communication capability are worth the expense especially during prolonged maintenance or construction activity.

Slick/Wet Surfaces
Slip and fall potential and wet surfaces are an unescapable reality of confined spaces and underground construction. Yet these conditions are still predictable and can be lessened through

such things are proper footwear, practiced movement, and pre-rigged taglines for prolonged activity. I have been in many penstocks with extremely slippery, slimy, silty surfaces, and yes, I've landed on my butt more times than I really want to admit. Another *fun* confined space to work in is tanks that store cooking oil. Of course, the tank is empty but the walking surface is slipperier that black ice. With these types of predictable surface conditions consider shoes with soft rubber and aggressive tread. In the case of food manufacturing and containers and tanks like the one I just mentioned, sterile PPE may be required. Consider rubber boot overlays with non-slip treads. Include the discussion of short, side-step walking techniques during a pre-entry tailgate meeting. Consider knee and elbow pads for the inevitable *slip-up*. When a slip and/or fall may lead to a fall greater than four-feet fall protection must be provided. Be advised, the use of a tagline might be used as a travel restriction, however, the tagline does not qualify as fall arrest system unless the connecting anchor has been rigged to meet OSHA fall arrest requirements.

Falling Objects

Accidental dropping of objects into a confined space has been the source of many serious injuries and fatalities. Managing work over the top of an active confined space entry is critical and must be highly regulated. This safety requirement applies not only to work done directly over the top of the opening, it also applies to top-work taking place in proximity to the opening. In the spirit of Murphy's law, if something is dropped nearby an opening it always seems to find its way into the hole! A single ½ lb. nut has approximately the impact force of 600 lbs. when dropped into a 300' vertical shaft. A direct hit on the helmet of a lower-level worker in this scenario would result and a serious neck injury and possibly death. OSHA fall protection criteria would apply in this case, including, but not limited to the use of netting above the hole. The best solution is; no work is allowed above an active confined space vertical entry.

Claustrophobia

Claustrophobia is the overwhelming fear of being in enclosed or confined spaces. One may think that these individuals would not be in confined spaces. For the most part that would be correct, however, the few cases I've witnessed were actually one of the rescue team members! If indeed you think you might be claustrophobic speak up. There is no shame in honesty. The fact is, there are plenty of extremely important jobs to do outside the hole.

Stored Energy

Even though the host employer and all workers feel that a proven lockout/tagout program is in place sometimes less-obvious conditions exist that may catch the entrants by surprise. In this case I am referring to stored energy typically associated with equipment and tools. This may also include equipment failure. A notorious example is pneumatic pipe plugs.

Below is a study I wrote at the request of a company that was involved in a pipe plug explosion in an underground construction site. This accident resulted in a compound fracture of a worker's arm. (The company name and accident location has been omitted for the privacy of the parties involved.)

Pneumatic Pipe Plug Failure Supplemental Analysis Study by Pat Rhodes

As with all major accidents, there are usually several indicators/factors/red flags that may predict the impending accident. These indicators and factors may range from the time of day, scheduling deadlines, and worker training; to the environmental situational awareness, subject matter knowledge of the task and subject matter knowledge of the equipment being used. Whereas all of the factors are extremely important and should be addressed, this analysis makes no judgment on any host employer, contractor, subcontractor, and/or employees. *The focus of this analysis is simply on the failure of the pneumatic pipe plug in question.*

Factor 1 – The age, make and model of the plug:

Manufactured by SAVA, this is a municipal grade, flow-through-bypass plug. It is designed for pipes 6" to 12" in diameter at a *maximum* inflation pressure of 36psi. Based on the model number, 912917 and visual inspection of the photos, this would appear to be an old plug that may no longer be in production.

Factor 2 – Questionable modifications to plug's inflation valve and bypass valve:

This plug appears to have been modified with a Chicago quick-connect ball valve and extended with approximately a 3" long copper pipe for the inflation port. This extension pipe seems to have been added to allow the modifier room to turn the handle. Typically, this type of pneumatic pipe plug is manufactured by SAVA with an Industrial Interchange nipple factory attached to the unit. The bypass valve has been modified with a simple household type hose bibb valve. The manufacture requires an *Industrial Interchange* quick connect water coupler.

These highly unusual and questionable modifications make remote manipulation of the valves virtually impossible, thus tempting the user to reach in the pipe to manipulate the valves. Additionally, the 30-degree angle of the hose bib valve threads contributed to the difficulty of reattaching the bypass drain hose prompting a manual (hand-in-the-pipe) manipulation of the pneumatic pipe plug.

The purpose of the factory required connectors is that they can be attached and detached at a safe distance with the remote placement adapter with a telescoping aluminum pole. Additionally, at no time should workers be allowed to stand in front of an active inflated pipe plug. This is a true blast zone proportional to the amount of head pressure in the pipe.

Factor 3 – Monitoring a pneumatic pipe plug that has been left in a pipe for an extended period of time:
These plugs are designed for temporary pipeline blocking. Per the manufacturer's requirements plug pressure must be checked at least every 5 hours during extended inflation. This particular pipe plug was reportedly placed in the pipe and left inflated for close to 24 hours without inspection. Did the original installers perform the manufacturer mandated safety inspections?

Factor 4 – The condition of the interior pipe surface:
As stated by witnesses, it was decided that the surface needed to be roughed up to give a suitable surface for good paint adhesion. As such, the pipe plug was being repositioned deeper into the pipe to be out of the way of the grinder. What was the condition of the pipe surface at this deeper repositioned location?

Per the manufacturer's requirements, the pipeline should be properly cleaned, all sharp particles removed in order to prevent poor sealing and decrease of back pressure values as well as possible damages of the pneumatic plug.

Factor 5 – Unknown and/or excessive plug inflation pressure:

During the repositioning of the pipe plug, using a high-pressure air-compressor tank (approximately 120psi), inflation levels for this failure were *estimated* and never verified with a reliable pressure gauge in close proximity of the pipe plug.

With the exception of some high performance/stainless steel pneumatic pipe plugs, this type of municipal grade plug requires a relatively low inflation pressure of 36psi applied with only a manual hand or foot pump and approved pressure gauge.

Predicable Outcome:

- Given a 12" pipe plug, and head pressure of 36psi, the total head pressure on the plug equals approximately 4,068 pounds. It should be noted that head pressure of this particular plug in question was not determined.
- Given a 12" pipe plug over inflated to a failure point of 120psi, the total head pressure and subsequent projectile impact force of the failed plug could have equaled as much as 488,160 pounds.

The manufacturer warns that over inflation may cause a rupture of the plug resulting in serious injury, even death.

Personal Note:

The basis of this analysis is through the research of the product operating manual and the product website (www.savatech.com), and my years as a rescue specialist and instructor for FEMA, AZ TF-1 and Phoenix Fire Department. As a rescue specialist, I used pneumatic lifting bags, pneumatic shoring and pipe plugs for trench rescues, heavy equipment rescues and building collapses. I was required to complete basic pneumatic physics and advanced technician training for the use of these powerful tools. During an actual rescue in Phoenix we successfully freed a man trapped under the axle of a railroad boxcar by lifting the boxcar with pneumatic air bags inflated to 36psi.

End of Analysis

A.I.R.

(Assessment, Isolation, Resources), the role of Incident Management during a confined space emergency

The role of the Incident Manager is one of paramount importance. The actions of this person will most likely determine the success, or failure of a confined space emergency. There are two major concerns that will determine ultimate success or failure of the rescue operation.
1. Safety of the rescue team members.
2. Overall efficiency of an event that will be brought to a successful conclusion.

Regardless of who is attempting scene control, the employer or the fire service, it is essential that we recognize a confined space environment when we are not expecting one. Many potential rescue locations are not legally permit required confined spaces. However, I have always strongly believed in treating every rescue potential as if it were a confined space emergency. This includes all the rope access and tower rescue jobs I've been involved with. Towers are indeed confining places; they have limited space to work, they are not intended for continuous human occupancy, they have limited means to get on and off of, and they usually have something dangerous on top, not to mention the extreme fall hazard. The similarities to confined spaces must not be overlooked. The tallest tower I've done rope work on was 980 feet. Ironically, the highest rope job I've personally did was a true permit required confined space...a 1,200-foot vertical shaft.

WE MUST TAKE THE BLINDERS OFF AN LOOK AT THE BIG PICTURE!

The Incident Manager must deal with three areas of action, and it must happen, for the most part, simultaneously. These areas of action apply to standby rescue jobs as well. When called upon for a standby rescue job these areas of action should be identified in advance and documented in a formal rescue plan.

- A complete and accurate ***assessment*** of what happened (or what could happen during a standby), who is in charge, and what are the hazards.

- ***Isolation*** of the area, and all hazards, anything that may cause harm to the public, the victims, and to our own people.

- Identify and call for the appropriate ***resources***.

Assessment

Two Most Common Pitfalls

It may not be reported as a confined space emergency. Many employers push the limits of reclassifying confined spaces as non-permit required, thus allowing alternate entries. By doing this, they eliminate the need of the daily permit process for lengthy jobs. This simple fact tends to slow down the notification and response of a rescue team. Whatever the case, we must recognize the presence of a confined space and plan for the appropriate rescue response, regardless the classification.

They look safe. Directly related to the first pitfall of reclassification, most confined spaces people get injured or die in look safe. That's probably the reason the victim went inside the space in the first place and the same reason the would-be rescuer entered to save his buddy! If the confined space had a rattlesnake in it no one would go in. Keep that mental image in your head of a rattlesnake waiting to attack in the next confined space you enter. Maybe, that will lessen the effect of complacency when entering a simple space.

The victim is down for a reason, don't become another victim by making an ill-thought-out rescue, even for a fellow rescuer. If it got him/her, it will get you. **What you don't see may kill you.**

What happened?

Competent Person/Supervisor, Responsible Party, Witnesses.
What happened? The first responder should try to identify who is the responsible person. If the space is located on an industrial or construction site, there will most likely be a Competent Person, or Entry Supervisor close at hand. *Keep that person with you at all times during the rescue!* These resources can provide valuable information on what happened, what hazards have been identified, the possible location of the victim, and the layout of the confined space.

Other witnesses, co-workers, and friends may also provide needed information as to what happened.

What are the hazards?

Onsite Entry Permit.

An important diagnostic tool during a confined space emergency is the entry permit. OSHA 1910.146 general industries standard on confined space is the driving force for the mandatory use of entry permits during a permit required confined space entry. OSHA does not publish a standard entry permit. It is up to the company to create their own legal form that addresses these areas of importance.

- The permit space to be entered
- The purpose of the entry
- The date and the authorized duration of the entry permit
- The names of the entry supervisor, attendant, and entrant(s)
- Identification of any potential hazards
- Identification and conformation of the lockout/tagout of the space
- The results of initial and periodic atmospheric testing
- The rescue and services that will be summoned in the event of an emergency
- The communication methodology to be used by the entrants and the attendant
- Any other notable safety and health information specific to the space to be entered
- Identify required equipment, such as communication, PPE, and rescue that must be onsite

Note: The primary focus on the study is rescue. I will not be addressing the development of entry permits, alternative entries, or reclassifying confined spaces in this book. For additional information and guidance on these and other related permit required confined space topics visit the OSHA website at: https://www.osha.gov .

Victim Profile

Rescue or Recovery?

The first responder should determine how many victims have been affected. We should try to determine how long the victim(s) have been down, the mechanism of injury, and the survivability profile of the victim. As soon as safely possible, a decision must be made as to whether the operation will be run in the *rescue or recovery mode*. During the rescue mode safe expediency may be justified. However, during a recovery mode all rescue (body recovery) activity much be slow, deliberate and well planned.

Isolation

Control access to the area.

People of good intention will try their best to squeeze in as close as possible to the opening of the space, to get a peek, or to help. Do whatever it takes to keep them back a safe distance. Call law enforcement early for crowd control. *Use hazard line tape, it works!* Controlled access is not only important for bystander and rescuer safety, it has the positive effect of giving the rescue team enough mental room to make important critical decisions.

Hot, Warm, and Cold Zones

Accountability zones are a must. Create a hot zone, warm zone, cold zone. The distances between each zone will depend on the nature of the emergency, including but not limited to: vertical fall hazards, potential for IDLH atmospheres, the stability of the surface, and the crowd factor.

Hot Zone

The Hot Zone is ground zero, the location of the actual rescue. No one should be allowed inside the Hot Zone who is not directly involved with the hazard zone entry and victim extrication. Accountability is the point of entry into the Hot Zone. Entry into the Hot Zone is strictly enforced by the *Accountability Officer*.

The diameter of the Hot Zone is established by Command based on the following key factors:
1. Type of emergency – i.e. hazmat vs. tower rescue with downed lines, a hazmat emergency may require an entire building to be designated as the Hot Zone, whereas downed electrical lines may require a Hot Zone diameter of 500'.
2. Location – Is it in an open field or a location more confining like electrical vaults or trenches?
3. What is the number of rescuers and equipment required to work within the Hot Zone.

Warm Zone

The Warm Zone is the emergency support area surrounding the Hot Zone. Typically, the Warm Zone extends 50' beyond the outside boundary of the Hot Zone. Again, this is a command decision based on location and support needs. The Warm Zone includes *Level One Staging* – staging of immediate needs resources.

Cold Zone

The Cold Zone is the non-emergency support area surrounding the Warm Zone. Typically, the Cold Zone extends 50' beyond the outside boundary of the Warm Zone. Again, the spacing of the zones is a command decision based on needs.

Command Zone Scheme (Typical)

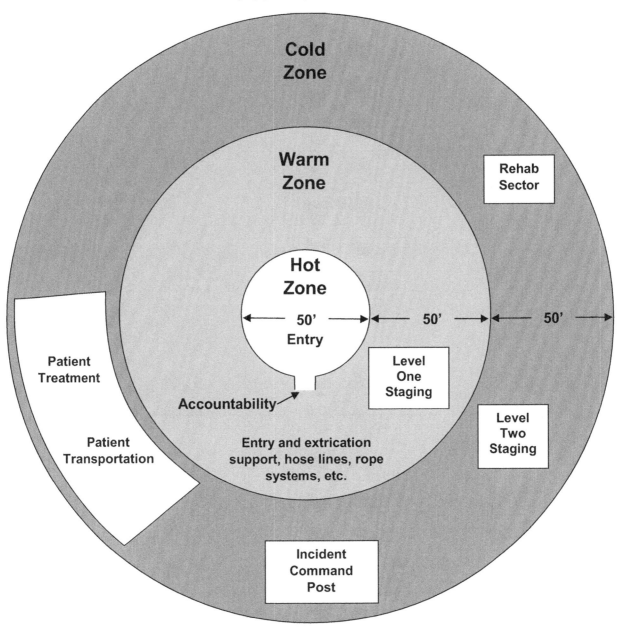

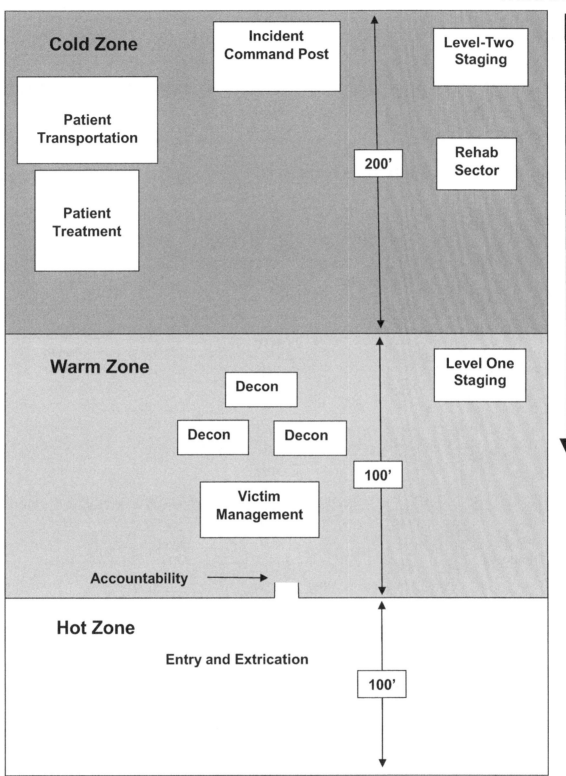

Lockout, Tagout

Confined space Lockout/Tag-out (LOTO) Considerations

The lockout/tag-out (LOTO) phase of a confined space entry is most often the first item of business. This can be as simple as throwing a breaker and putting a lock on the breaker box, or, as complex as locking out a hydro-electric plant at a dam that will have a LOTO room and a LOTO supervisor. This may include water-flow clearances that would require notification of any number of electrical facilities in the region. One can only imagine the catastrophic flooding that could happen with a single mis-step. Rest assured, there are a number of thumbprints and checks and balances for such an event. It's the less complex and routine confined space entries that tend to encourage complacency and possible shortcuts on the lockout-tagout requirements. These worry me the most.

During a rescue event all LOTOs should be re-confirmed. Regardless of how small or unimportant the entry may be perceived; the rescue team should promote the same level of urgency that would be expected at the hydro-electric facility. Some places of employment actually add a third component to the Lockout and tag-out. They label it "Try out". In other words, after the LOTO is declared complete, they will try to turn the hazard source on. Nonetheless, verification by all parties involved in the LOTO is an absolute must. Do not take the word of a single individual the confined space is safe. Insist that they show you and explain to you the LOTO process is valid. Is the LOTO process above your head? That's okay...still have them explain the process to you. It must be right before entry.

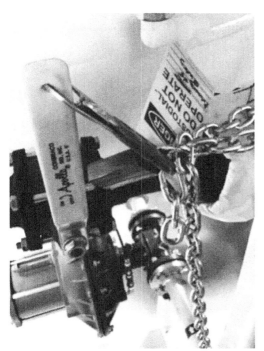

> The lockout/tag-out process on any job can be complex, however, all parties involved in the confined space entry, whether it be the workers or the rescuers, are entitled to know that the space is indeed safe to enter and work.

Atmospheric controls such as gas valves, and air handling systems may provide great use for isolating atmospheric conditions. All utilities associated with a confined space involving a rescue must be accounted for. Any liquid product or engulfment potential related to the rescue area must be locked-out and verified through the tagout process that the hazard potential is eliminated. All manufacturing or rescue site-related equipment hazards must be de-energized and certified void of any stored energy. *In addition to written tags, padlocks and other physical restraints should be used went possible.*

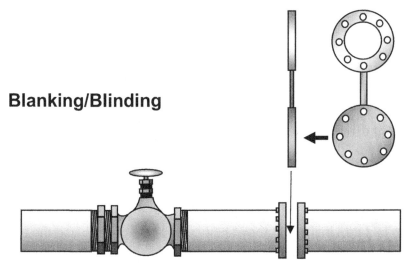

Blanking/Blinding

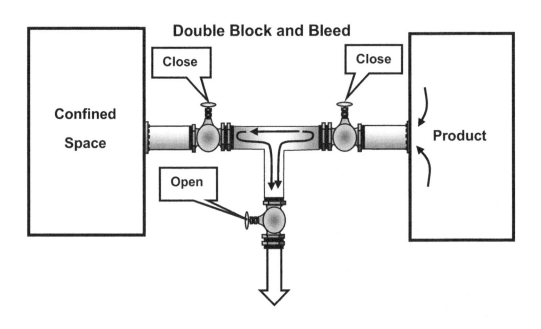

Double Block and Bleed

Atmospheric Monitoring

Atmospheric hazards are the number one killer in confined space emergencies. Because of this, confined space emergencies are usually as much a hazmat incident as it is a rescue incident. Rescue units should be equipped with four-gas atmospheric monitors, hazmat units will have the same, plus colorimetric, and any number of appropriate and specialized atmospheric monitoring equipment. If you don't have immediate access to an atmospheric monitor, your best action might be to sectorize, and keep a safe distance from the space.

For the first responder the *onsite entry permit* may be the best early clue to the condition of the atmosphere of the space. This is only a pre-rescue indicator; the rescue team must always rely on their own monitoring equipment to verify atmospheric conditions.

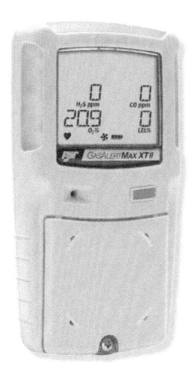

Trigger Alarm Points for a Four Gas Meter

O_2: 19.5 Low - 23.5 High

LEL: 10% (of the calibrant gas)

H_2S: 10ppm.

CO: 35ppm

Normal Air

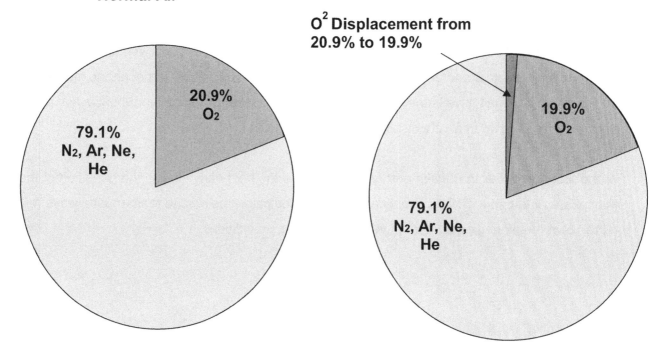

How bad is a 1% displacement of O_2 on the air monitor?
Keep in mind that 19.9 is not low enough to trigger the alarm.

Equals a total air displacement of 5% or *50'000 PPM*

This is due to the fact that the O_2 sensor of the monitor is accounting for only 20% of the air content that is oxygen. It would hold true that the remaining 80% not being accounted for would also be equally displaced.

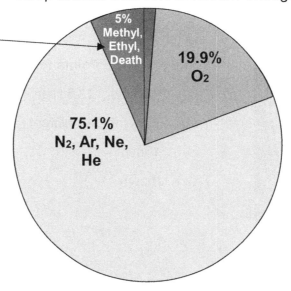

LEL (Lower Explosive Limits), and UEL (Upper Explosive Limits)

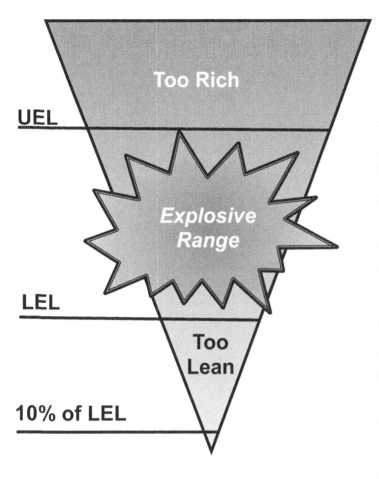

All flammable vapors have an explosive range. Any mixture of air and vapor that is above this range is said to be too rich to explode. Any mixture of air and vapor below this range is said to be too lean to explode. Additionally, atmospheric monitors are typically calibrated to either Pentane and Methane. Although these two gases are a close *guesstimate* of many other flammable gases, it is not an exact science. When a known flammable gas is being metered with a four-gas meter use a cross-reference LEL chart to determine that exact LEL. These charts are numerous on the internet and the manufacture of your monitor may very well have their own version.

Vapor Density

Vapor density is the weight of a gas compared to an equivalent amount of air. Air is equal to 1. The vapor density of Kerosene, is (4.7), its vapors will drop to the lower levels, whereas ammonia is (.596), and it wants to rise. Vapor density is most notable in vertical spaces. However, low level O2 displacement from heavy vapors has been an insidious death trap in spaces as shallow as five feet. Diligent multi-level atmospheric monitoring should be a key task for all confined space entries.

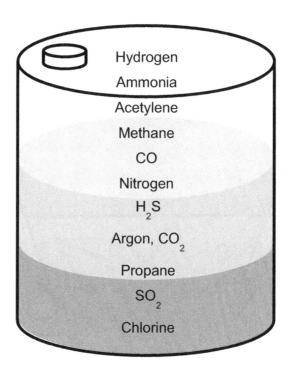

Hydrogen
Ammonia
Acetylene
Methane
CO
Nitrogen
H_2S
Argon, CO_2
Propane
SO_2
Chlorine

Testing All Levels

- Verify that the sampling hose is clean and dry and void of any pinholes.
- Lower and raise slowly at a rate of about 6 inches per second.

Resources

First Responders: Call for Technical Rescue and Hazmat early.

This early command upgrade is equally important to the fire department first responder as well as industrial in-house rescue teams. The first benchmark in the command process of a confined space emergency is the awareness that the situation is potentially beyond the available skill sets of the first responder. Get the technical rescue and hazmat big guns rolling early, you can always turn them around if it turns out to be something that can be handled by the responders already onsite.

1. Determine if there is an adequate number of trained personnel on scene to do the rescue/recovery. This can vary greatly depending on the hand that command was dealt, and whether it is a rescue mode or a recovery mode. A confined space rescue needs to be resolved pretty fast (yet maintaining safety), whereas a recovery will automatically bring everyone out of the woodwork, including law enforcement and probably OSHA investigators. A well-established command will greatly enhance both modes.
2. Command should consider the effect of temperature extremes on personnel, and consider early rotation of personnel operating on scene, approximately every 15 to 20 minutes, 30 minutes in the winter.

Proper equipment and trained personnel is critical to safely complete the operation. This includes, but is not limited to:
1. Atmospheric monitoring equipment.
2. Ventilation equipment with the necessary duct work.
3. Explosion proof lighting.
4. Explosion proof communications.
5. Personal protection equipment.
6. Supplied air breathing apparatus or remote air.
7. Victim removal systems/equipment.

When needed, call for law enforcement early for traffic and crowd control.

Ventilation

Not all confined spaces are compatible with mechanical ventilation, however, when ventilation can be provided, either for work or rescue, it can provide a much more tenable environment for the entrants. Open-ended systems such as storm drains and sewers are particularly stubborn in maintaining a healthy atmosphere due to a more continuous flow of water and contaminants. Atmospheres in non-continuous, enclosed structures as seen with tanks and other storage vessels are easily improved with a quality ventilation system.

Ventilation for an unplanned emergency response will vary greatly in comparison to a planned rescue standby job or work performed in a confined space. During a planned entry there is enough time to effect multiple atmospheric exchanges. Typically, I will try to get seven air exchanges within the space for a planned/work related entry. For an unplanned rescue you might be lucky to have any ventilation at all! Determining one air exchange is simple to calculate. Treat the space as a cube, even if it's shape is cylindrical. Multiply the height x length x depth, then divide that total by the CFM of the blower. Of course, this will render a total area greater than the cylinder, but we're erroring in our favor.

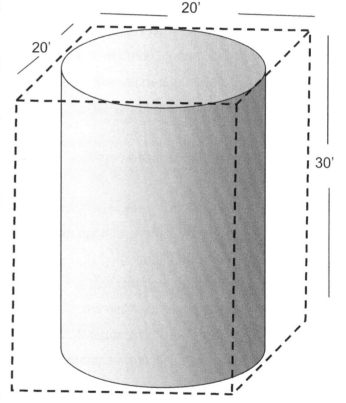

20 x 20 x 30 = 12000 cubic feet
12000 (Cubic feet of space) divided by 1600(Cfm of the blower) = 7.5 minutes (one air exchange)

Ventilation may be positive (blowing in) or negative (sucking out). Either way, it is important to monitor the air quality going in and coming out. Rescuers have been known in a few cases to have place their blower in close proximity to the exhaust of their running emergency vehicle and filling the space with carbon monoxide! It should also be noted that negative ventilation should be avoided when potential explosive environments are in the space. A simple static charge of explosive vapors traveling through the ductwork could result in an explosion. Intrinsically safe blowers and ductwork are available for potentially explosive confined space environments.

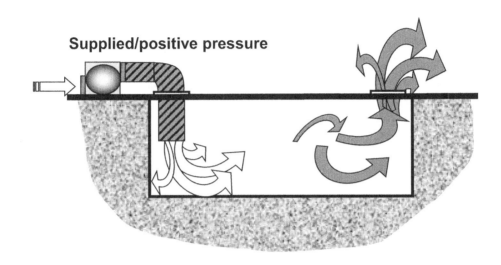

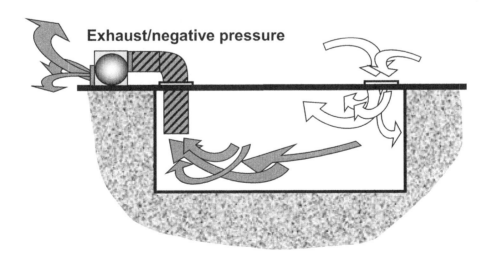

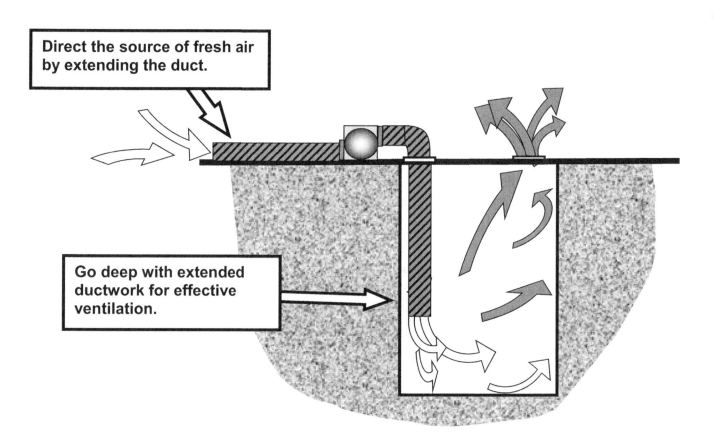

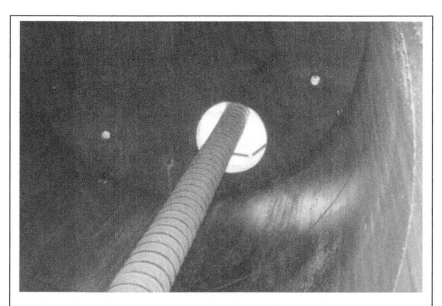

Ventilation is most effective by getting the ductwork as deep as possible in the confined space.

Personal Protective Equipment

Best practices for confined space rescues typically require entry and back-up personnel to wear the proper level of personal protective equipment. This usually includes helmet, gloves, proper footwear, goggles, class III/full-body harness and applicable respiratory protection. However, some spaces are configured in such a way conventional confined space rescue PPE might present a hindrance to a safe entry. A quality pre-plan must include these PPE considerations.

Chemical Protection

Does the rescue involve the extrication of workers involved in cleaning activities within the confined space structure? This could be an endless array of conditions, such as; resin tanks, polymer tanks, or waste water treatment. Whatever protective clothing barriers the entrant/victim is wearing, the rescuers must be equipped with at least the same level of PPE. Often, due to the nature of the emergency, the rescuers may need to don chemical suits that is a higher level of protection than what was originally mandated for the entrants working in the space.[ii]

Breathing Apparatus: There are several considerations concerning the use of breathing apparatus in a confined space:

1. OSHA 1910.134 – Respiratory Protection, mandates that an employer provide respiratory protection to each employee when such equipment is necessary to protect the health of such employee.
2. Is the rescue a non-planned reactive response, or a planned entry?
3. A reactive response is typically what the fire/rescue service will see. In such cases, most fire services are ultra-proactive in donning their SCBAs as soon as they get on the scene not really knowing what type of atmosphere they're dealing with. Indeed, the probable root cause of their response is most likely an IDLH atmosphere.

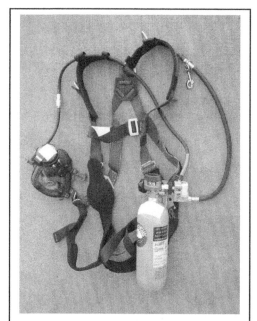

Scott supplied air harness, emergency egress bottle and face piece.

4. Planned confined space entries most often will focus on making a non-IDLH work environment prior to any employees entering the space to perform work. As such, the employee may not be required to have respiratory protection. However, as we all know all too well, and verified by NIOSH, the vast majority of confined space fatalities are attributed to spaces that someone deemed safe to enter! Presented with even the slightest potential of an IDLH environment, entry and back-up personnel should be prepared to don SABA (supplied air breathing apparatus) or SCBA when making entry into a confined space.
5. What is the configuration of the confined space? Like all PPE taken into a confined space, SABA vs. SCBA is highly dependent on configuration of the space itself. What are the dimensions? Does the horizontal distance and/or the vertical depth exceed 300 feet? The maximum allowable distance of hose line for SABA systems is 300 feet.
6. If entry personnel use an SCBA, they must not enter any farther than one half the amount of supplied air minus approximately 500 lbs. EXAMPLE: 2000 PSI tank gauge pressure--1/2 = 1000 PSI minus 500 PSI = 500. In some cases such as lengthy underground construction projects pre-placed fill stations may be called on for the purpose of refilling SCBA bottles within the space. Another option for exceedingly long entries is to pre-stage additional SCBAs and bottles.

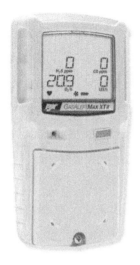**Air Monitoring:** Best practice is for all entry personnel to use personal air monitoring devices that monitor O_2, flammability, and toxicity, however, this isn't always possible or practical from a manpower prospective. A good rule of thumb is to have one monitor for a maximum four workers within a pre-determined same level area. The safety supervisor needs to stay on top of this supervision and maintain strict accountability of workers within this pre-determined area. Known and/or potential hazards will play a major role in pre-planning the approved area of work.

Communications: Unless line-of-sight or simple use-of-voice is a reliable method of communication, entry personnel should have a minimum of one portable radio and/or be equipped with a hard wire intercom system. A common fire service practice is for the first entry team member be equipped with hard wire communication and an air monitoring meter, the second member should have the tag line and a portable radio, this way the portable radio is less likely to accidentally key the air monitor.

Staying with the common theme of quality pre-plans, communication consideration must also be included. There should be no communication surprises when working a confined space. I have been involved in a number of underground locations such as storm drains, penstocks, sewer systems, and other underground waterways. Some of these were miles in length. In some of these extra-long and/or bending locations we were able to maintain radio communication by pre-planning and installing repeater antennas throughout the tunnel system.

Confined Space Extrication and Rigging

Confined Space Rigging Equipment Considerations

Rigging equipment in the rescue world is in a continuous state of evolution. Keeping abreast of the latest and greatest must-have-rescue-toy can be overwhelming, time consuming, and, even obsessive. Regardless of the current equipment marketing trend, some equipment considerations never change. These elemental considerations are driven by the same core rigging physics that propels our entire industry. Additionally, due to the universally binding need for safety in the vertical environment plus the mandate for expediency during a vertical rescue event, some rope rescue equipment has been proven to meet our needs better than others.

Most certainly, given a high level of journeyman rigging skills, most vertical rescues can be successfully completed with a bare minimum of equipment. However, if we stay steadfast in our belief that rescue is indeed a trade, than we must be willing to invest in the tools of the trade that will promote safe and expedient work.

This section of this book will explore a few key considerations of rigging equipment within the framework of safety, expediency, and rigging physics compliancy.

Rope

Through much of my career in the fire service, ½ inch, static kernmantle rope was the mainstay for main and belay lines and most everything else in-between. We were all caught up in the old NFPA 600 lbs., two-person load, bigger is better fear tactic. As time went by, my questioning of such directives became more embolden. Rescue environments such as towers and structural steel and backpacking rope for wilderness applications really influenced a lighter more efficient justification for the use of 11mm rope. With the growth and modernization of rope access I became completely sold on using low stretch and/or static 11mm or smaller diameter cordage. As of today, I harbor a disdain for ½ inch rope. It's fat and clumsy to handle and it is completely dysfunctional as a usable rope access tool. Being that rope access skills are paramount for the vertical agility that I promote for successful rescue rigging techniques, ½ inch rope has no place in my equipment cache.

The argument that ½ inch rope will account for rigging mistakes or unforeseen mishaps is a strong indicator of unconscious incompetence. The fact that the fire/rescue community adheres to a standard (NFPA 1983) that divides rope rescue equipment between *General Use* and *Technical Use* sometimes empowers inadequate rope skills. In reality, if a team cannot perform at a high technician level than they are only ready for incipient non-entry rescues and should not be considered for major vertical rescues. Sounds hard and radical? Sorry, there will be no sugarcoating on this belief from me.

All rigging factors are predicable to a true rope access and rescue practitioner. There are no surprises in rope rigging when the actions are based on sound physics. It is very doable to obtain high safety margin with the use of 11mm rope by a qualified practitioner, whereas, an inadequately trained rescuer can easily reduce the system safe factor to dangerously low levels using ½ inch rope in combination with poor training (or no training) in applied rigging physics. To thinks ½ inch rope will cover the ignorance of an inadequately trained team is a lethal miscalculation.

Carabiners

Using the strictest definition of OSHA fall arrest criteria and ANSI z359, carabiners are classified as connectors. Why is this important? Today, with the advancement of industrial rescue teams, we are seeing more of a trend in rope equipment compliance with these important fall arrest standards. Here are a few factors that should be considered when choosing carabiners for your team. In addition, I'll also address a few best practices for the use of carabiners:

Without exception, a carabiner is designed to be loaded on its major axis. Having stated this, the definition of "major axis" will vary based on the shape and design of the carabiner. The axis of the typical "D" shape carabiner is easily visualized as being down the spine of the carabiner. Whereas the major axis of an oval shape carabiner will bisect the center of the carabiner frame but still parallel to the spine. Some devices such as the Petzl ASAP must be used only in conjunction with an oval carabiner that allows for a wider loading of the major axis and minimizes potential binding that would be present if a "D" shape carabiner were to be used. As with all equipment, adherence to the manufacturer's recommendations will usually surpass most equipment standards.

Several rescue carabiners do have a minor axis rating as well as an open gate rating stamped on the spine of the carabiner. However, this is done more as a warning of how not to use the carabiner as opposed to condoning dangerous practices. Depending on the make and model, side loading and open gates dangerously weakens the strength of the carabiner.

It is correct to say that carabiners are not designed to be side loaded, but we all are aware of weak rigging practices such as sloppy knot craft is seen all the time. As such, the rescue community builds in some aspect of safety margin into the manufacturing of equipment. The most common solution to the prevention of gate loading is maintaining small gain to the connecting loop of the knot. A great knot for *non-loaded* ropes, such as some belay lines is the double overhand noose. This knot cinches tightly around the carabiner maintaining spine loading when using a non-tensioned rope. A word of warning, if the double overhand noose becomes loaded it can be next to impossible to untie!

This shows a Double-Overhand Noose connected to a non-loaded carabiner for the purpose of a belay line jumper (providing belay redundancy for the floating directional pulley.

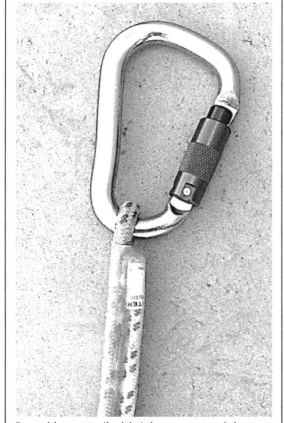

Bound-loop prusiks (shrink wrap around the stitches) are fantastic for maintaining a firm loading of the major axis of the carabiner.

As to standard interpretations, the latest ANSI z359 version now requires a 3,600 lbs.-minor axis for a fall arrest connector. As of November 18, 2016, OSHA 1910.140, Personal Fall Protection Systems, also adopted a minor axis rating of 3,600 lbs. for carabiners. On the flip side of this topic, NFPA 1983-2017 appears to distancing themselves from the OSHA and ANSI 3,600 lbs. minor axis mandate; NFPA 1983-2017 – Technical use carabiners major axis is MBS-22kN (4946 lbs.); and minor axis is MBS-7kN (1574 lbs.); General use carabiners major axis is MBS-40kN (8992 Lbs.) and minor axis M73BS-11kN (2473 lbs.). Note – per NFPA 1983-2017, 1.3.3, this standard shall not apply to industrial fall protection for general industry and construction.

Why is a working knowledge of these standards important? Depending on which hat your wearing you might not be compliant with some of your equipment. Rope access and confined space workers typically need to be compliant with OSHA fall arrest criteria, whereas rescue personnel might be more in tune with NFPA. What is obvious is that there are substantial safety margins built into all of these high-quality rescue products. A good round number for a safety margin promoted by the fire service is somewhere close to a 10:1 for anchorage and connectors. ANSI z359 is the only current *consensus* standard that states a safety margin specifically for rescue anchorage and that is five times the intended load.

The term "stage" is sometimes used to defined the number of movements it takes to open a carabiner. 2-stage, and screw type carabiners are still widely used without no abundance of adverse effects. Having said that, the 3-stage versions are almost impossible to open accidently, whereas, on extremely rare occasions, 2-stage versions have been known to open due to rolling contact with a foreign surface such as another rope. Screw gate carabiners are fine for most rescue applications, but due diligence must be given to the gate so that the closing end is pointing down when in use and that the gate is indeed screwed close. This action allows gravity to help keep the gate from unscrewing. It should be noted per OSHA fall protection criteria that only auto-locking connectors are approved. As such, screw gate carabiners are no longer allowed for general industry personal fall protection applications.

What is the pros and cons when comparing steel carabiners with aluminum carabiners?
Types of high-quality rescue carabiners currently on the market are vast in numbers. This includes steel and aluminum alike. The obvious difference is their weight. Mountain rescue teams or tower rescuers are much more incline to backpack aluminum carabiners and lighten their load by several pounds.

In terms of the rated strength, the ratings will vary widely depending on makes and model. The tensile strength of steel will run between 36kN (8,100 lbf) to as high as 70 kN (15,750 lbf). Aluminum will typically run between 25kN (5,625 lbf) and 36kN (8,100 lbf). Consider the intended load as well as the rescue environment. Even with a hypothetical large rescue load of 500 lbs., the lightest rated aluminum rescue type carabiner will still offer you close a 10:1 safety margin.

When looking at steel versus aluminum, as you might guess from my comments on ½ inch rope, I greatly favor the use of aluminum carabiners. Like ½ inch rope, steel carabiners are fat and clucky when attempting rope access work. Although the minimum breaking strength of aluminum is slightly less that steel, a strong argument can be made that aluminum carabiners are more durable due to shock loading flexibility of aluminum versus the rigidity of the steel counterparts. The bottom line is that aluminum is streamline, light weight, and efficient. Extremely high safety margins are easy to maintain with aluminum carabiners when combined with the applied rigging physics of a true rope access and rescue practitioner.

Descenders

Friction control devices (descenders) have been around as long as rope. Today, there are a zillion descent and friction control devices on the market. They can be as simple as adding a bunch of wraps around a tree or as complex as the MPD. All of them accomplish their goal of applying friction to descend at a controlled speed. Friction control is a key physical component in rigging. We're trying to overcome friction during the hauling process, and we're trying to use it to our advantage during the lowering process.

Fixed or Traveling[iii]?

What anchor position options are there for descending? There are only two options for rigging a descent device. It can be at the FIXED position at the anchor or it can be at the TRAVELING position on the person descending.

The *Fixed* position at the anchor is always used during team-based operations when the load is being lower by another individual who is controlling the descender. With the fixed position it should be noted that the standing part (the rope bag) is up by the anchor and the working end (end of the rope coming out of the bag) is tied to the load.

Whereas with the *Traveling* position, the descent device is attached to the individual who is descending (rappelling) and in control of the device. The rope bag (standing end) is over the edge and the end of the rope is tied to the anchor on top.

Friction Management

Friction control of these many devices is done by bending the rope and creating a greater composite angle of contact between the stationary device and the moving rope. Example: if a rope is lowered over a simple 90-degree wall there is a 90-degree angle of contact; when you apply two round turns of the rope around a handrail there is 540 degrees of contact (hence the reason behind the name of the 540-belay device). A six-bar brake rack will apply approximately

720 degrees of contact when fully loaded, the more you squeeze the bars together the greater the angle of contact and the slower the load will move until it simply stops.

This friction stuff is all fine, but what makes a good friction control device?
1. The device should be simple to learn and easy to use. I prefer the Petzl I'D for most rope access and rescue applications due its intuitive friction control handle, ease of learning and overall durability and reliability.
2. The rope should bend through the device in an in-line fashion as opposed to a curling or coiling fashion. Curling the rope under tension (especially with kernmantle static or low stretch rescue rope) tends to introduce curling and tangling memory into the rope when it becomes unloaded (kind of like curling ribbon with a scissors when wrapping a present). This is a rope maintenance problem with devices such as a rescue eight or various manufactured forms of tubes.
3. It should be manufactured by a recognized company with a history of quality products and reliable support.
4. The device should have a proven history of high performance and customer satisfaction.

Rope Compatibility

Will descenders work on any type of rope? What about the rope diameter?

Brake racks typically work well with either ½ inch or 7/16-inch rope (11mm). However, racks are quickly loosing favor to the Petzl I'D and the CMC MPD because these devices are so useful and easy when converting a lowering system to a hauling system. The Petzl I'D is outstanding and a highly recommended device for rope access and rescue. The MPD is outstanding as a progress capture device for a conversion from a lowering to a hauling system. However, both are rope diameter dependent. For ½ inch (12.7mm) rope you must use Petzl I'D L (Red), likewise for ½ rope you must use the Red MPD. For 7/16 (11mm) rope you would use the Petzl I'D S (Gold), and for the MPD you would use the Silver 7/16 (11mm) version.

ANSI z359.4

Given the compliance concerns of general industry rescue teams and well and the fire service, descenders should meet the requirements of ANSI z359.4-2013. In short, this standard states that descenders must auto stop when the operator lets go of the device, and that it must have an anti-panic auto function.

What is "anti-panic"? An anti-panic feature is typically associated with friction control descent devices. These devices have a friction control handle that when over pulled or activated the device will auto-stop. This allows the user to simply reset the handle and continue at a more controlled speed. Most descent devices do not have this type of feature and when the control handle is pulled wide open you will fly whether you want to or not.

Intuitive vs. Counterintuitive

The normal human reaction to falling is to grab and hold. Given a descent device that is compliant with ANSI z359.4-2013 and has an engineered anti-panic feature, a descender that is intuitive in its design has a control handle that plays into this grab and hold human reaction causing activation of the panic stop function.

As stated above, I prefer the Petzl I'D for the best performing descent device that incorporates an anti-panic feature. The handle is extremely intuitive in its design. When the operator panics, grabs and pulls the handle the Petzl I'D will stop. Some devices, most notably the MPD, are counter-intuitive. To activate the auto-stop of the MPD while in the descent mode the operator must let go of the "T" handle. In a panic state of mind (even for a nanosecond) having to let go of something goes against every human sensibility when someone is falling. Test have proven time and again that a nanosecond of hesitation is worth several feet of freefall!

Rope Grabs

What is a rope grab and what types of rope grabs are available? What are the advantages and disadvantages of each? To answer this question, we must first define rope grabs. In rigging, a rope grab is a device that holds the rope in place or as a means of holding and pulling the rope. Not all rope grabs are suitable for belay/fall arrest applications. In other words, rope grabs are not synonymous with belay or vertical fall arrest devices. Some devices might qualify for both mainline and belay line functions under specific applications.

The term Progress Capture defines a function of a rope grab that is rigged to the mainline anchor.
- Example, the Petzl I'D is commonly used as a progress capture component of a haul system, it is therefore holding the rope (load) in place while allowing the haul team to re-set the system. The Petzl I'D also qualifies as an approved belay device simply by the activation of the same internal mechanisms under a shock load event.

The types of rope grabs available in today's market are too numerous to count or list in this publication, however, we can define two major divisions of rope grabs: 1) Soft rope grabs, and 2) Hard rope grabs.

- Soft rope grabs are made of rated textile products such as prusik loops tied or stitched 6mm-8mm cordage or less common, webbing loops. These loops are tied to the host rope using a prusik hitch or one of a number of other approved hitches.
- Hard rope grabs are manufactured devices such as the Gibbs Ascender, the Petzl Rescucender. There are many.

Advantages and disadvantages:

- Soft prusik loops and webbing loops are light weight and easily backpacked for wilderness use as well as some sport climbing applications and industrial applications as seen during tower work. These same loops (depending on their rating) may be used for quick and reliable anchorage. A basket hitch from a webbing loop is a quick and effective anchor point when atop a steel tower. Many of these stitched loops have ratings that are as strong, if not stronger than the carabiner that will be connected to them.

  One disadvantage to soft loops is that they tend to really bite the host rope when used at the hauling position and need to be physically loosened to facilitate a re-set of the pulley system. Additionally, rope climbing with prusik loops is doable, however, due to the same biting effect, extremely cumbersome for most people. Some hitches such as the French Prusik, or the Caver's Helical Knot, or the Valdotain Tresse Hitch (VT Hitch) are used to provide a quicker release when used for climbing.

- Manufactured hard rope grabs are very reliable and extremely quick to release and reset. This reason alone is why mechanical hand ascenders and foot loops combined with a mechanical chest component such as a Petzl Croll is a must for any rope access job or any time rope climbing over a few feet is required.

  There are not many disadvantages to hard rope grabs other than they might be a bit more clinky hanging on your harness and they weigh a little more than those prusik loops. At no fault to the hard rope grab, some people thing that all hard rope grabs qualify as a belay device. This is a very dangerous assumption! Unless specifically approved by the manufacture as a belay device, the majority of hard rope grabs are not designed to be shock loaded and should never be used as a belay.

Will a rope grab work on any type of rope? The answer is, yes, no, and maybe. As it has been stated above, there are a million and one rope grab combinations out there. Each one has its own characteristics and design function. This question is highly dependent on the type of rope and the rope grab device. Soft rope grabs (hitches) tend to be more universal however there is the tendency for more slipping to occur the closer the diameter of the prusik loop is to the diameter of the host rope. Hard rope grabs are mostly universal when using ½ inch rope or 11mm (7/16-inch) rope. Although a few rope grabs are specifically design for one diameter of rope only. Strict adherence to the recommendations of the manufacturer is required by all users.

The new Petzl Rescucender get's my editor's choice award for rope grabs. Petzl has eliminated the old pin format and replaced it with this innovative auto-lock/quick release version.

Can a rope grab cut a rope if too much stress is applied? Yes. Usually too much sudden stress is the result of a shock loading event. This is why most rope grabs are not designed for belay/fall arrest applications. When simply hauling or climbing, the potential of shock loading the host rope with the rope grab is exceedingly rare. Most rope grabs, soft and hard alike, will start to slip long before serious damage can occur to the host rope. This slippage of the rope grab can be equated to a fuse in an electrical system. When overloaded, the fuse (rope grab) will slip and the system will lose power. When the haul prusik slips, this is a strong indication that the load is too big, or, as seen more often, there is too much surface contact causing excessive friction on the haul line, or possibly the system has been rigged wrong. Figure it out and fix it!

What are the advantages of sewn prusik loops compared with tied prusik loops? Sewn prusik loops are manufactured and certified, tied prusik loops are not. Many brands of sewn prusik loops choke the loop at the stitch point with shrink tubing. This is a great option for clipping a carabiner to the loop. By using the shrink tubing to choke the carabiner, we promote correct loading of the spine and greatly reduce the chance of side-loading the gate of the carabiner. This is more of a problem for traditional tied prusik loops where the carabiner loop is big and floppy and carabiner side-loading is a common occurrence.

Opinion on Standards Interpretation

Manufacturers continue to develop new gadgets and tools for work and play in the vertical realm. This whole manufacturing phenomenon has greatly influenced standards development. Although federal and state laws address working at height safety parameters and vertical work positioning, historically, manufacturers are the most active in promoting rope access and rescue standards. For a manufacturer of rope access and rescue gear, active standard development is extremely good business. A growing number of rope access and rescue practitioners believe these product driven rope access standards are gospel. In my opinion, at least in the United States, the broad-based regulations of OSHA are the most important and readily available guidance for safe practice in the vertical, and confined space environments. Additional international consensus standards that are well written and applicable to general industry rope access are ISO 22846-1 and ISO 22846-2. Cal-OSHA has now passed into state law the first rope access standard; Subchapter 7, Group 1, Article 4, 3270.1. Use of Rope Access Equipment. Many believe, (myself included) that this is a precursor to a dedicated rope access standard in OSHA.

All too often companies, department, and agencies will take volunteer/consensus standards such as *NFPA 1983-2017, Standard on Life Safety Rope and Equipment for Emergency Services:* or *ANSI/ASSE Z359.4-2013, Safety Requirements for Assisted-Rescue and Self-Rescue Systems, Subsystems and Components* and include them in their own standard operating procedures as a "Shall" compliance statement. By doing this, you have just taken a volunteer standard and made it legally binding for your agency.

OSHA regulations are unquestionably mandatory laws in the United States, whereas consensus standards such as ANSI, ASTM, and NFPA are not. Consensus standards do play a major role in OSHA regulation development. They may have a say in some civil litigations, and are very useful as a reference guide. Having a strong understanding of the content found in applicable consensus standards is highly recommended – just don't paint yourself into a corner by making them a mandatory named inclusion of your team's standard operating procedures.

Knotty Thoughts for Confined Space Rescue

Anyone who know me know that I'm a knot nut. I've never seen a well tied knot that I didn't like. However, I am also extremely opinionated on the use of the right knot for any given application. In this section I've selected a few favorite knot tying practices that may be of some use in work and/or rescue. I've written quite a bit on the subject of knot tying essentials in a couple of other books; *A Practitioner's Study About: Rope Rescue Rigging* and *Rhodie's Guide to Rescue Knots*. I would recommend that you take a look at these books for greater details on knot craft.

Elements of a Knot

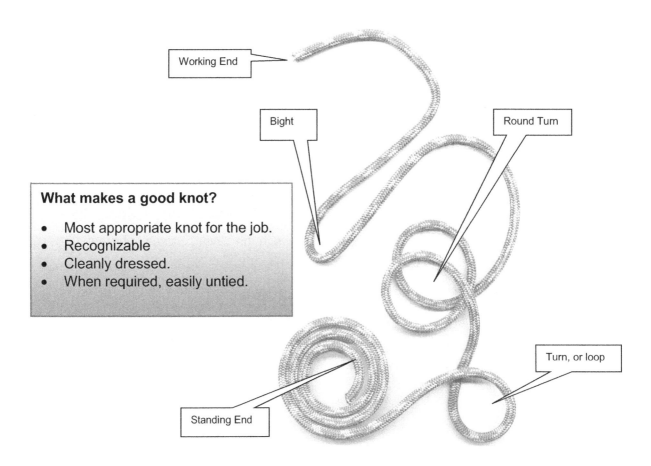

What makes a good knot?

- Most appropriate knot for the job.
- Recognizable
- Cleanly dressed.
- When required, easily untied.

Clove Hitch

Hitches are a type of knot that, for the most part, is dependent on a host object for maintaining its form and function. When the host object is removed from the hitch, or the hitch is removed from the object, the hitch will come apart. The Clove Hitch exemplifies the true meaning and usage of a hitch.

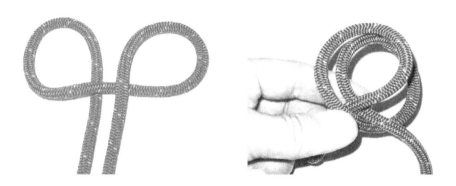

Clove Hitch Tied Around an Object

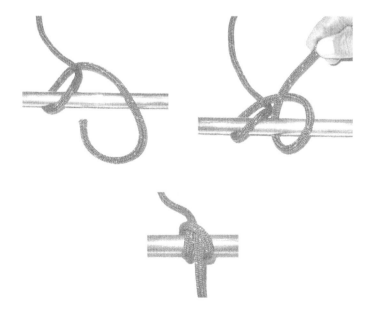

Prusiks

The Prusik is used in everything from personal attachment points for ascending, to system uses such as Tandem Prusik Belays, and Haul Prusiks for mechanical advantages. The ability to tie the prusik correctly is a must for all rope rescue personnel.

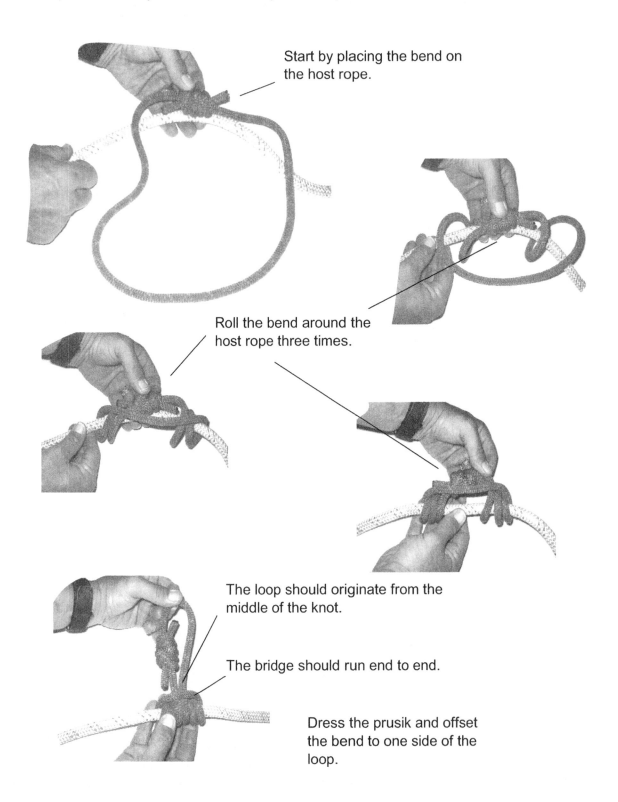

Start by placing the bend on the host rope.

Roll the bend around the host rope three times.

The loop should originate from the middle of the knot.

The bridge should run end to end.

Dress the prusik and offset the bend to one side of the loop.

Some Thoughts On the Bowline

Without question, my favorite category of knots in rope access and rescue is bowlines. The variations of the bowline run easily into the hundreds. It is also important to acknowledge the historical importance of the bowline family as it applies to rigging. The name itself is derived from the line use to secure the bow of a ship – the "bow line". There are few knots that can compare to the bowline that can accept extreme tension and still easily untie after the tension is released.

The basic Bowline may be analyzed as having two components. One component is a bight at the working end, and the second component is a half-hitch located at some point mid-line. We use half-hitches all the time to secure items for hauling such a pike-poles and other tools. The use of the half-hitch on the tying of the Bowline is very much the same principal. In the case of the Bowline, the half-hitch is securing the bight as it is weaved around the standing part of the line. Or if you prefer (From your Scouting days as a youth): The rabbit (working end) comes out of the rabbit hole (the half-hitch), runs around the tree (the standing part), and dives back into the rabbit hole (the half-hitch) …whatever floats your boat, just as long as it comes out correct!

Front Profile

Reverse Profile

The Yosemite back-up (Yosemite Bowline) is nothing more than taking the working end of the knot and retracing the original half-hitch component (the rabbit hole) of the original Bowline. When completed you will have two parallel half-hitch components.

Portuguese Bowline

Using this knot craft methodology, the Portuguese Bowline is tied by employing the "Snap-Bowline technique.

By mindful of the dressing and placement of this adjustable leg which is common between both anchors.

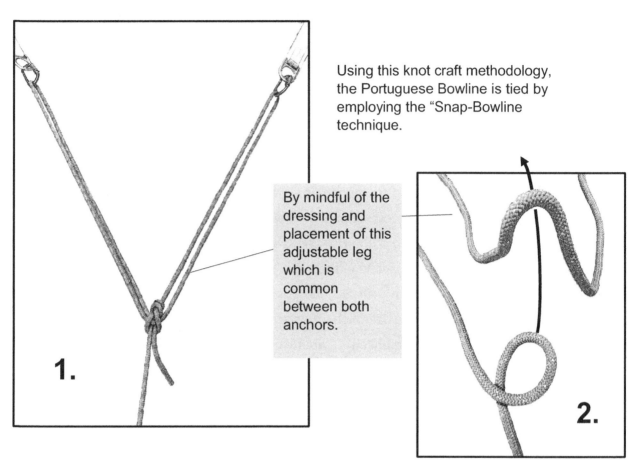

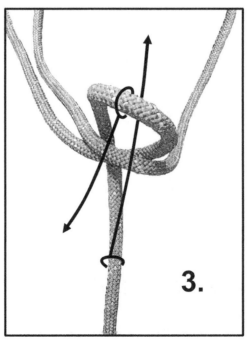

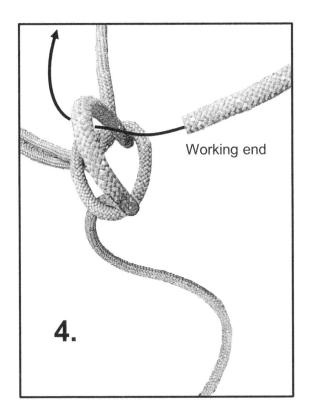

Working end

4.

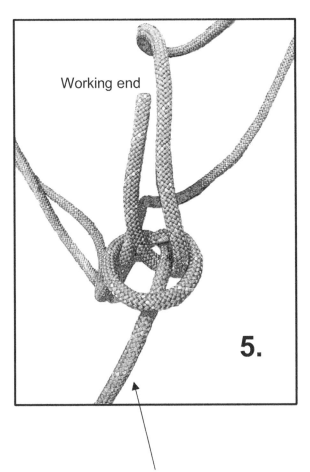

Working end

5.

Pull the Standing end to invert the slipped overhand into a

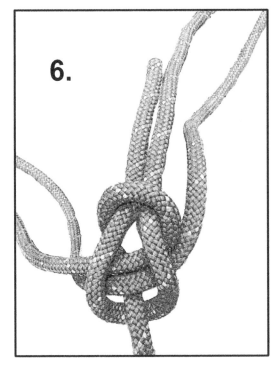

6.

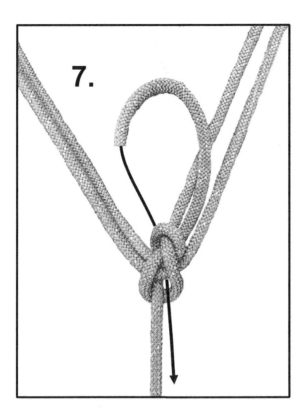

Finish the knot with a Yosemite backup.

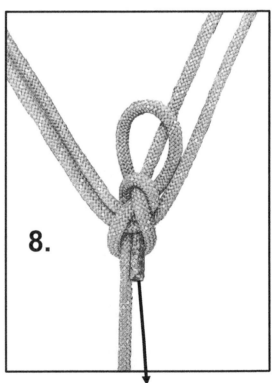

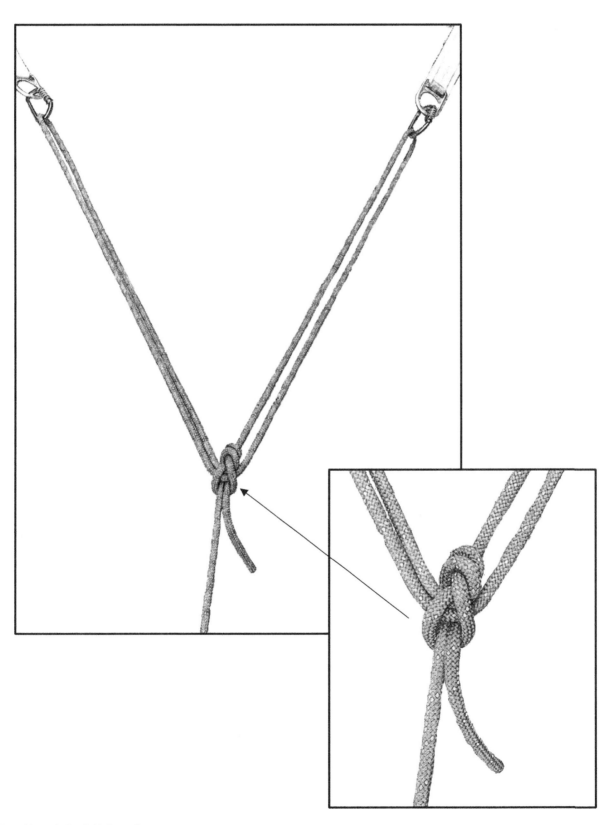

Butterfly

The Butterfly is the most versatile mid-line loop. This knot is very fast to tie, quick to untie, and easily recognized.

In addition to its mid-line qualities, the Butterfly has three distinct loops, when the knot is opened up, can be loaded in three different directions.

It is considered part of the overhand family, and it is a close cousin to the "Ashley Bend", the Striate Bend and the "Hunters Bend".

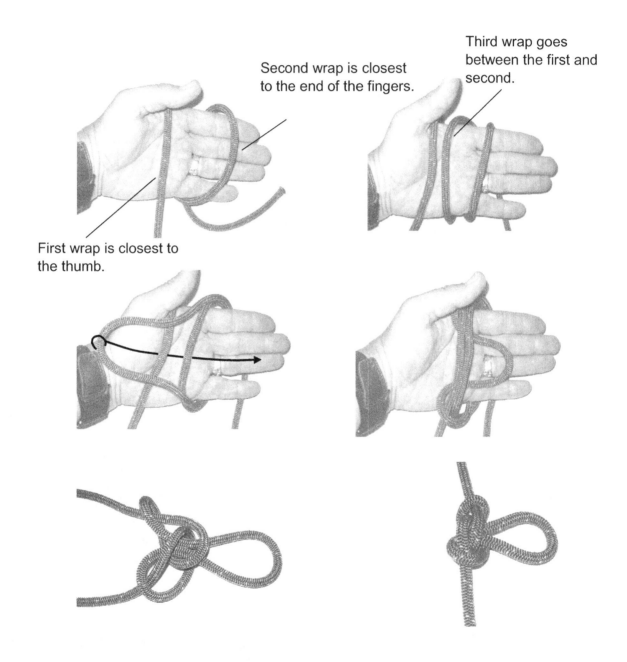

Butterfly Tied from a Bight (Twist Method)

Many times, it is preferable to tie the butterfly from a bight, this technique allows for a precise location of the final loop. This is a valuable tool when rigging multiple tensioned back-tie anchors as shown in the bottom photos.

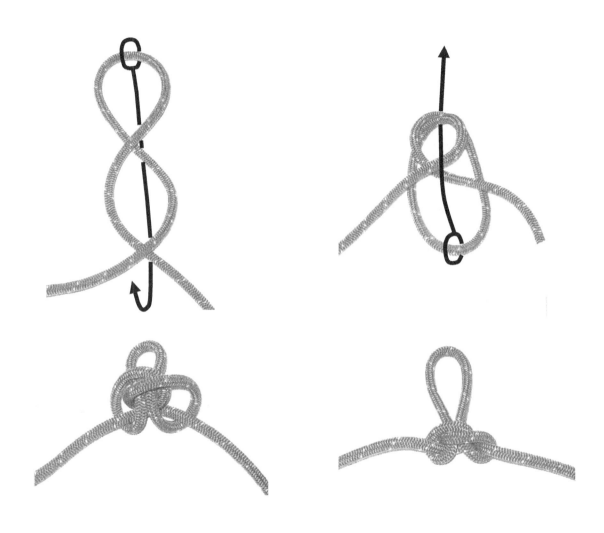

Figure Eight Family

Even though I am usually tying bowlines, Figure Eight knots will always be a mainstay for rescue knotcraft. Most specifically; the Figure Eight on a Bight, and the directional Eights (Inline Eights). At times I am fond of using a Directional Eight to create and Two-Loop Figure Eight equalizing system. The following pages on the Figure Eight Family will focus primarily on Directional Eights and the Two-Loop Figure Eight.

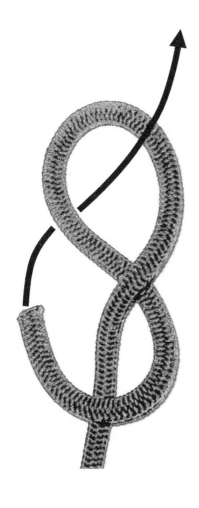

Directional Eight or Inline Eight

Another knot from the family of eights, the Directional Eight is very useful as the first step of an unequal Two Loop Figure Eight Follow Through (next page). This knot has lost some appeal as a midline knot for me personally because I do not feel it is as functional as the Bowline with a Bight, the Butterfly, and the Clove Hitch. Some of the inherit flaws with this knot is that it is extremely hard to untie after heavy loading, it may capsize if pulled the wrong way, and many people have problems tying it correctly.

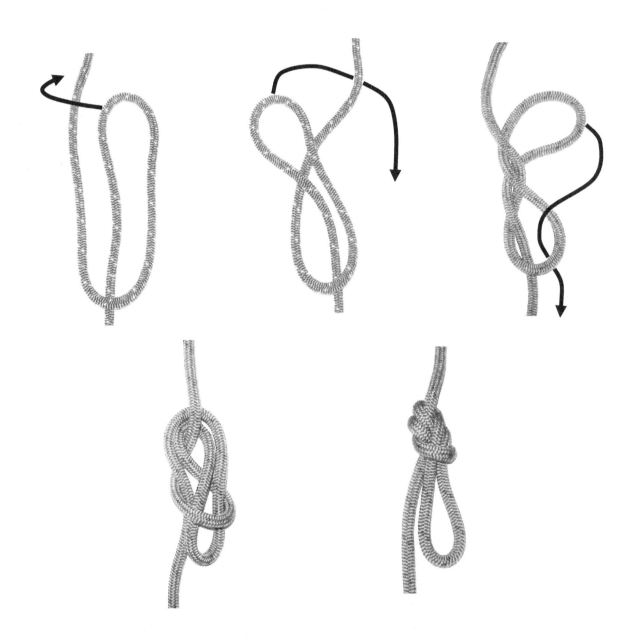

Unequal Two Loop Figure Eight Follow Through

This knot is a great way to construct an equalizing anchor system with the working end of the rope. I have found this knot to be especially useful in making a control rope connection to the front of a rescue raft during a boat-base operation.

There are two basic knot skills required in forming this knot: first, correctly tying a Directional Eight, and second, correctly performing a follow through (retrace) of the Directional Eight.

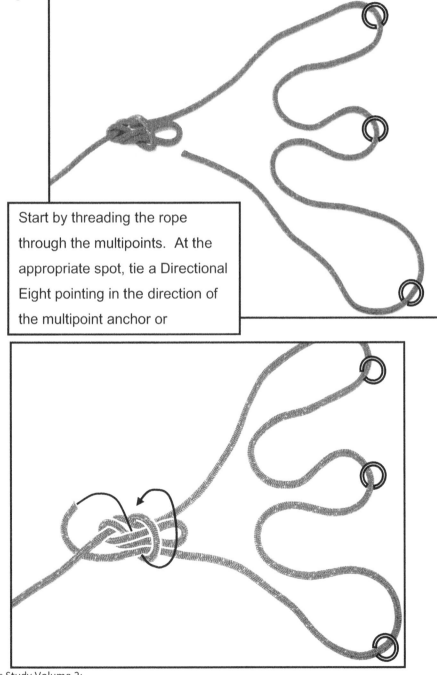

Start by threading the rope through the multipoints. At the appropriate spot, tie a Directional Eight pointing in the direction of the multipoint anchor or

Start and complete a retrace of the Directional Eight as shown here and in the next three steps.

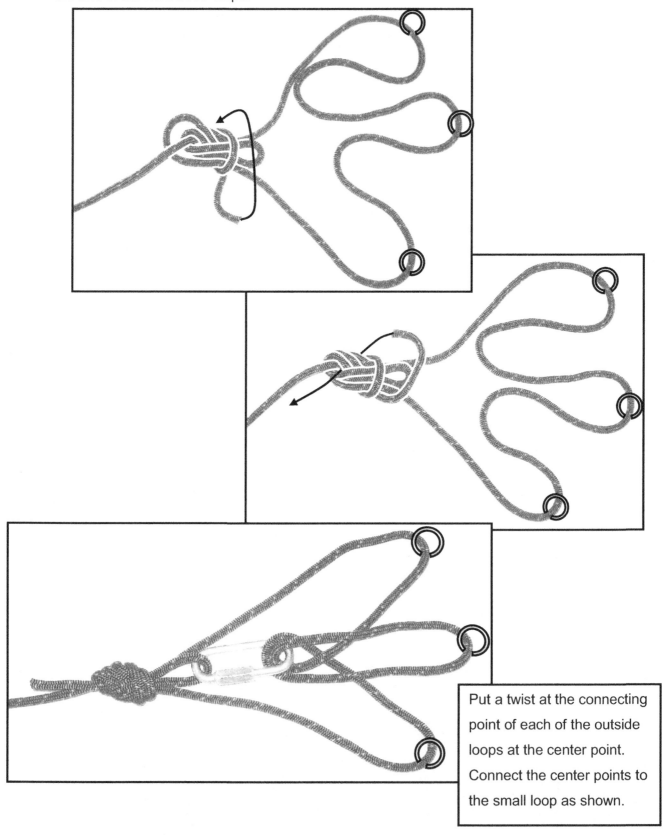

Put a twist at the connecting point of each of the outside loops at the center point. Connect the center points to the small loop as shown.

Lowering/Raising Tools In/Out of Confined Spaces[iv]

Taglines are common to the fire service for hauling tools to roof tops and other high points. Taglines work in the same manner when lowering or raising tools in and out of confined spaces. Probably the most preferred combination of hitches for this purpose is a Clove Hitch and a Half Hitch.

The Clove Hitch is typically tied at the bottom of the tool and one or more Half Hitches are tied towards the top.

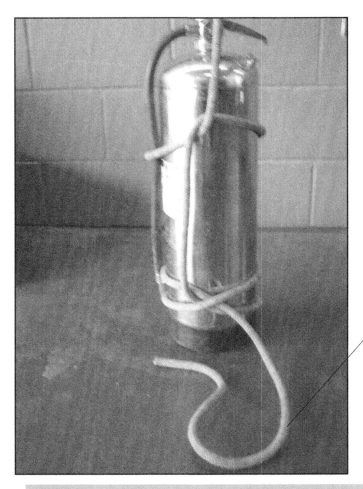

When the middle of the rope is used to tie the tool, the bottom end of the rope may be used as a tagline to clear obstacles during the lowering or haul.

Safety Note: This combination of knots is very effective; however, extra care is always required when lowering any item into a confined space or lower level where workers and/or rescuers might be present. No one should ever be underneath items involved in vertical movement. If needed, vacate the lower level and omit the use of the bottom tagline.

In this example, an axe is vertically moved by the same combination of a Clove Hitch and a Half Hitch.

Note that the head of the axe is additionally secured with a loop from the Clove Hitch.

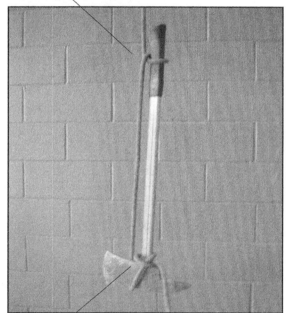

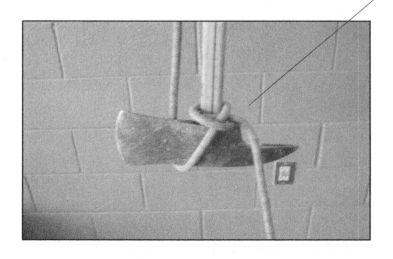

Rescue Anchorage Considerations for Industry

As stated earlier, this book is an extension of my previous book *A Practitioner's Study About Rope Rescue Rigging*. This section on rescue anchorage is a discussion on the legal interpretive considerations of rescue anchors and how that might affect the selection of anchors used in the urban/industrial rescue world. For greater details concerning anchor *rigging* please refer to *A Practitioner's Study About Rope Rescue Rigging*

What does "bombproof anchor" mean? In my years coming up through the ranks of various rescue teams I was typically taught that a bombproof anchor was an anchor that everyone on the team would agree was indeed indestructible, and that we could hang the world from it. Anything less than that would be considered a marginal anchor…however…if you connected an appropriate number of marginal anchors together you might be able to produce a bombproof anchor…providing that everyone on the team would agree. Wow! That was kind of like the old adage; if you don't know how to tie a knot than tie a lot. Furthermore, who's doing the choosing of the anchor, what is the criteria for the anchor selection process, and who is performing the anchor rigging?

To shed a bit of light on this bombproof/marginal anchor thing let's try to distinguish between an anchor and an anchor system. Again, as historically taught, the anchor is the thing, item, and/or structure that we might choose to connect our anchor rigging to. A marginal anchor might be a catwalk in a factory, or a small pine tree in the forest. Whereas the bombproof anchor might be a large "I" beam in the factory and possibly a large, 20 ton bolder in the forest. The anchor system is typically thought of as the combined rigging that we attach to the anchor that allows us to connect our other rope goodies to.

I have always had a aversion for this terminology. I tend to lean more on the OSHA term 'anchorage". Anchorage implies both; the anchor thing plus the rigging we rig to the anchor thing. Regardless how big and impressive the anchor thing is if the rigging attached to the big thing is subpar then we have nothing. Conversely, through the use of proven and physically sound rigging techniques, we can take a marginal anchor (or no anchor at all) and create a substantial, reliable system that accommodates the intended load plus precisely dictate the anchor location.

If you could assign a minimum rating to anchorage what would it be? 10,000 pounds? 6,000 pounds? Maybe 3,000 pounds? OSHA now mandates that the anchorage for a single person

(310 lbs. maximum weight) rope descent system shall be able to support at a minimum 5,000 pounds. Ultimately, the answer to this rating is that the anchorage must be able to support the intended load <u>plus all applicable force multipliers</u>. This means that the person responsible for the anchorage selection and subsequent rigging better be squared away on rigging physics. For those users who are less than qualified to make these calculations, they must be limited to the use of pre-determined and pre-qualified anchorage. Unfortunately, much of this anchorage selection process is made by well-intended, under-trained rescue or rope access team leaders who are not truly qualified persons. They simply do not know what they don't know about applied rigging physics.

Qualified Person vs. Qualified Decision

This is a good time to discuss what a qualified person is. A *qualified person* is defined by OSHA as one who, *"by possession of a recognized degree, certificate, or professional standing, or who by extensive knowledge, training and experience, has successfully demonstrated the ability to solve or resolve problems relating to the subject matter, the work, or the project."* This is not be confused with a *competent person*. An OSHA *competent person* is defined as *"one who is capable of identifying existing and predictable hazards in the surroundings or working conditions which are unsanitary, hazardous, or dangerous to employees, and who has authorization to take prompt corrective measures to eliminate them"* [29 CFR 1926.32(f)]. What does this have to do with anchors? In our growing field of rope access, the crossover of terminology and legal interpretations of federal and state safety laws pertaining to fall arrest systems is inevitable. This trend will affect the way we design anchorage for industrial rescue and rescue standby as well. In short, especially for rope access jobs, we need to use manufactured approved (and installed) anchorage. When this is not possible, then we must use an improvised anchor system that has been approved by a qualified person in the field of fall protection, rope access and/or industrial rescue.

Getting back to the qualified person definition stated above; these are all great qualities to possess by some of the leaders of your rescue team. However, there is a rich history of serious and sometimes fatal vertical accidents after the anchorage was approved by a 'qualified person'. I'm not as concerned with following the letter of the law as much as I am for having everyone go home safely at the end of the day. It should raise a red flag for all of us if one person alone has the final say over the suitability of the anchorage. I would suggest that we not rely merely on the reputation of one person, regardless of what degree he or she holds and/or how much experience this person may have, instead, rely more so on a *qualified decision*. A qualified decision takes into account the input of the qualified person. Conversely, and more important, the qualified decision must include a sound and understandable physical analysis of the anchorage, including the manner of use. Understandably, this type of analysis may not be as readily available while performing an un-planned rescue that may be experienced by a fire/rescue agency. However, there is no excuse for not having a qualified decision for anchorage involving rescue training, rope access, and rescue standby.

Qualified Decisions

A qualified decision on anchor systems for planned standby rescues, or long term training events may require a substantial amount of detail committed to a formal document. It may be a standalone document or it may simply be an explanation within a rescue plan or rope access rigging plan. Anytime a qualified decision is written it is justifiably a legal document in the eyes of OSHA.

On the next page I am showing a qualified decision case study I wrote that addresses anchors installed by a fire department rescue program. The department's name has been omitted out of respect for confidentiality.

This municipal fire department frequented a local mountainous city park to perform mid-wall pick-off training. Occasionally they were called upon to actually rescue a trapped climber using the same anchors in question. This particular mountainous park is located in a desert and lacks suitable wilderness type anchorage. Likewise, the geology of the rock terrain is very flaky and offered few options for quality anchors. Due to these limited anchor options this fire department decided to install strategically placed anchor bolts, paired, one belay and one mainline. The bolts chosen were Chicago 28 eyebolts that could be screwed into epoxied sleeves and removed when the job was completed. The sleeves were camouflaged with a removable cap to discourage public use.

The Chicago 28 eyebolt has a ¾" shank and it has an *inline pull* Working Load Limit (WLL) of 6,000 pounds with a minimum breaking strength of 30,000 pounds. It would appear to most rescue riggers that these numbers exceed any definition of a bombproof anchor. What the team leaders failed to understand is that any eyebolt is drastically weakened when it is *not* loaded inline. In this application, these anchor eyebolts were always loaded at 90° to the shank of the bolt…a worst-case scenario…and a direct violation of the manufacturer's user requirements.

Anchorage Qualified Decision Case Study Opinion by Pat Rhodes
Department name and location has been omitted to respect confidentiality

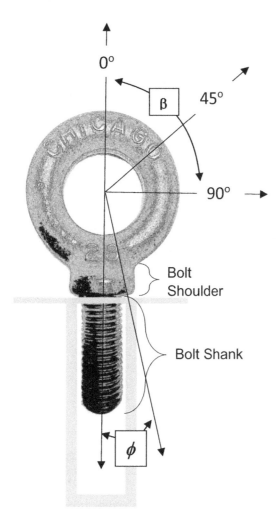

Per the manufacturer, Chicago Hardware and Fixture Company, the working load limit (WLL) for the Chicago 28 Shoulder Eye Bolt is 6,000 lbs. when pulled inline (0 degrees). When pulled at 45 degrees the working load limit is reduced to 1,500 lbs.

90-degree loading is not permissible per the manufacturer.

Typically every training evolution and rescue that has used these eye bolts are loading the bolts at the non-permissible angle of 90 degrees.

Chicago Hardware and Fixture Company does not list the working load limit at 90 degrees in their catalog, however by using the formula below the working load limit at 90 degrees can be determined to be 1,044 lbs.

Given that the bolt is seated correctly and there is no degradation of the epoxied sleeve, this rating at 90 degrees will support a 500 lbs rescue load with a minimal safety margin of approximately 2:1. However, given a mainline failure during an edge transition, and the 500 lbs load free falls three feet, the Chicago 28 bolt supporting the arresting belay line would conservatively sustain a shock load of at least 3,000 lbs. This would generate 17,241 lbs. of torque to the head of the bolt shank.

As such, a complete system failure could occur.

Stress to the shank of the eye bolt $= \dfrac{(M)(\sin \beta)}{\sin \phi}$

β = the angle created by the resultant component of the applied force and the vertical axis of the bolt *(critical angle of concern is 90°)*.

ϕ = the angle crated by the compression of the bolt's shoulder and the vertical axis (10°).

M = the *magnitude* of the applied force (The inline WLL of 6,000 lbs. is used as the applied force to determine the 90° adjusted WLL.).

Manufacturer's Inline WLL = 6,000 lbs

$$\dfrac{(M)(\sin \beta)}{\sin \phi} = \dfrac{(6000)(1)}{.174} = \dfrac{6000}{.174} = 34{,}483 \text{ lbs.}$$

$\dfrac{6{,}000 \text{ lbs}}{34{,}483 \text{ lbs}}$ = 17.4% of WLL = 1,044 WLL when loaded is at 90°.

A Practitioner's Study Volume 2:
Insights Into Confined Space Rescue
© 2018, Rhodes

Additional Factors:

1. **Seating of the Eye Bolt**

   The eye bolt is typically hand tightened than backed out a ¼ of a turn to almost a half a turn for the purpose of aligning the bolt with the main and belay lines. Creating even the smallest of gaps between the shoulder of the bolt and the surface of the sleeve substantially reduces the compression support provided by the shoulder. This will cause greater torque and bending moment to the shank of the bolt than what is calculated in the previous equation. Conversely, if the bolt is tightened completely and is not in line with load the potential of an angular side-loading of the eye is a distinct possibility. This possibility is further intensified if it is associated with a shock loading of the belay line.

2. **Potential Degradation of the Sleeve**

   When was the last inspection of each of the epoxied sleeves? Depending on the type of glue used during the installation of the sleeves there will be shelf-life associated with the product. Equally important is the possible degradation of the rock surface the sleeves were installed in. This mountain park geology is notoriously flaky and unreliable for anchorage. Typically, epoxy bolting tends to help with the integrity of questionable rock surfaces, however, this is an assumption that should not be made. Detailed and regular accountability of the reliability of these sleeves is of the greatest importance.

   Any bolt system in rock, regardless if it is mechanical or glued, will over time and repeated use cone the rock (basically, creates a cone effect from the end of the shank to surface of the bolt installation). This may or may not be visible to the casual observer. The only clear method would be through pull test and analysis by a qualified person.

3. **OSHA, and ANSI z359 Compliance**

   OSHA and ANSI z359 compliance for fall protection in the rescue community has historically been hotly contested. Many rescue teams believing that general industry law somehow does not apply to the world of rescue. To further clarify this issue, as of November 20, 2017 the new OSHA fall protection laws that include rope descent systems went into effect.

1910.27(b)(1)(i)

Before any rope descent system is used, the building owner must inform the employer, in writing that the building owner has identified, tested, certified, and maintained each anchorage so it is <u>capable of supporting at least 5,000 pounds (268 kg), in any direction, for each employee attached</u>. The information must be based on an annual inspection by a qualified person and certification of each anchorage by a qualified person, as necessary, and at least every 10 years.

Note: Capable of supporting at least 5,000 pounds for each employee; this may be interpreted to mean the anchorage must have a working load limit of at least 10,000 for a two-person rescue load. Given a 90 degree pull the Chicago 28 eye bolt will only support 1,044 pounds. This is a critical deviation from these requirements.

1910.27(b)(2)(ii)

The rope descent system is used in accordance with instructions, warnings, and design limitations set by the manufacturer or under the direction of a qualified person.

Note: The manufacturer, Chicago Hardware and Fixture Company, does not allow the Chicago 28 eye bolt to be used in the manner this fire department has been practicing.

OSHA goes on to explain that the employer and "building owner" may be one in the same. The language interpretation between building and property ownership and property in the form of a city park is admittedly debatable. What is not debatable is that OSHA holds all employers accountable to provide a safe work environment for their employees. Emergency response is arguably a grey area. However, practice and training events tends to be more black-and-white when OSHA looks at any work environment, regardless of who the employer is. A good cross reference/interpretation is Permit Required Confined Spaces. OSHA does not hold fire/rescue services responsible for permits during a true confined space rescue. OSHA will (and has done so) fine a fire department for not following permit requirements while *training* in a permit required confined space. Fall protection interpretation for rescue vs. training would in all probability solicit the same response from OSHA.

Recommendations

1. Validate the integrity of the epoxied sleeves. This action should be performed by a qualified person, ideally a civil and/or structural engineer. This qualified person should

have knowledge of the geological makeup of any rock surface these bolts sleeves have been installed in.

2. Given that the integrity of the epoxied sleeves is acceptable, discontinue the use of the Chicago 28 Eye Bolt as a rescue anchor and replace them with a swivel hoist type anchor bolt.; typically, ¾" thread compatible with current sleeves. This swivel bolt must be certified to a working load limit of at least 5,000 pounds in any direction of loading. Approval of this usage must be obtained from the manufacture in addition to a qualified person in fall protection and rescue anchorage.

3. Consider additional back-tie bolts and/or single point anchors that meet a 10,000-pound working load limit for potential two-person rescue loads.

Design a curriculum that addresses all the issues and options specific to this type of anchor. The target audience for this curriculum should be twofold; 1) rescue technician, and 2) instructor development and support. Subtopics should include; OSHA Fall Protection, NFPA 1983 and ANSI z359 standard requirements, static/dynamic system safety factors, single and multipoint anchor skills, and applicable rigging physics for rescue anchor management.

<u>End of Analysis</u>

Anchor Interpretations Based on Work Environments

Anchors used for rescue purposes versus anchors used for standby rescue and confined space entry jobs seldom see eye-to-eye. OSHA might give the rigger a pass during a life and death rescue situations whereas in the world of standby-rescue rigging and rope access work (at least in the USA) anchor selection is becoming more of a target of OSHA and ANSI fall protection compliancy. Debate of do's and don'ts/pros and cons of rescue anchor selection and rigging is relatively easy compared to anchor selection and rigging in the judistical world of rope access and fall protection standards. In an attempt to make heads-or-tails of this often-misunderstood rigging topic I've divided the following anchor environment summaries into five subdivisions: 1) Wilderness Rescue Anchors; 2) Urban/Industrial Rescue Anchors; 3) Pre-planned Rescue Standby; 4) General Industry Rope Access Anchors; 5) Construction Rope Access Anchors. Each one of these five subdivisions have notable differences in their job application and the type of equipment used to rig the anchorage.

Wilderness Rescue Anchors
1. Light Weight Equipment – Typically one-inch webbing, or Dyneema slings, easy to backpack, and preferable for anchorage around trees and rock formations.
2. More Rigging Intensive – Wrap-three/pull-two webbing anchors, tensioned back-ties are more commonly used to stabilize marginal anchors.
3. Minimal governmental regulation unless it involves the jurisdiction of a municipal fire/rescue service.

Urban/Industrial Rescue Anchors

Includes structural steel environments such as towers and bridges.

1. Heavier OSHA fall arrest compliant equipment – Instead of one-inch webbing that requires more time-consuming knot craft (This is a major reason for not using one inch webbing in high exposure tower/bridge environments.) urban/industrial locations are best served by pre-sewn slings and anchor straps with steel "D" rings.
2. Less rigging intensive – due to a greater abundance of structural support options, however, great care is needed for edge protection especially around sharper steel edges and concrete.
3. More governmental regulation – typically falling under OSHA law and important standards such as NFPA-1983 and ANSI-Z359.

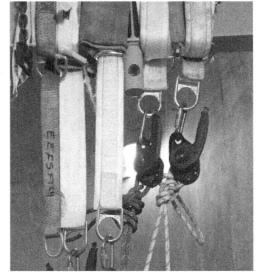

Pre-planned Rescue Standby

1. OSHA fall arrest compliant equipment – Hand-tied webbing anchors and untimely knot craft, once again, is not the best practice during this application. Stay with pre-sewn slings and anchor straps with steel "D" rings.
2. As with most industrial settings, steel and heavy structure components are usually available. Great care is still needed for edge protection around sharper steel edges and concrete.
3. Substantial pre-planning is still required – time to develop pre-plans is a distinct advantage when hired to provide standby rescue.
4. Anchors may be dynamically rigged to facilitate a rapped lowering or raising of a suspended victim.
5. Anchors should be approved by a competent person and/or a qualified person.
6. Standby rescue event are highly regulated by OSHA and are strongly driven by consensus standards.

General Industry Rope Access Anchors

1. Rope access anchorage is more reliant on the technical capabilities of the user. Even so, this anchor environment still falls under the regulatory control of OSHA.
2. The need for rope access may require more intensive rigging skills due to the advance nature of these type of jobs.
3. More than ever, pre-planning is a must – this type of event demands whatever time is needed to make sure the anchor engineering is correct prior to the start of any work.

4. As with the majority of industrial applications, dynamically rigged to facilitate a rapped lowering or raising of a suspended worker should always be considered.
5. Anchors may need to be approved by a qualified person.
6. Substantial governmental regulation – OSHA fall arrest requirements are strictly followed.

Construction Rope Access Anchors

1. The theme of heavier OSHA fall arrest compliant equipment is still the same. However, because it a construction environment, OSHA does allow some latitude in trigger heights for fall protection and the type of anchorage that may be used.
2. Rigging may be challenging; edge protection is a potential issue that cannot be ignored.
3. Pre-planning is critical, however, stay alert to changing worksite conditions that typically seem to pop-up at construction site.
4. Dynamically (ability to move and adjust in a highly controlled manner) rigged anchors are a strong consideration.
5. Improvised anchors must be approved by a qualified person.
6. Substantial governmental regulation – OSHA fall arrest requirements are strictly followed.

Belay Concepts Applied in an Industrial Fall Arrest World

Historically, belay systems, at least the way it has been taught by the fire/rescue services, was adopted from mountain/wilderness rescue back in the day. Tandem Prusik Belay Systems and Munter Hitches were (and still is in many fire departments) the go to methodology for belaying.

The basic definition of belay is to hold fast, or, to quickly stop. In early maritime England the act of belaying was mostly associated with holding a load; maybe by wrapping a cleat, or wrapping a bollard. Many of the rigging terms we use today had their genesis in early maritime language. Of course, in the modern rescue world, belaying is usually synonymous with a backup rope system, or as in industry and construction, a fall arrest system.

Today, belay systems have grown in interpretation and practice. With every accident or near mishap, a new interpretation and/or belay tool is bound to pop up. This single subject of belaying, or fall arrest continues drive the development and manufacturing of the wide variety of rope rescue equipment we use today.

Fixed vs. Traveling vs. Dynamic

The terms Fixed and Traveling[v] we used to describe descent device location may also be applied to belay devices. When I say *fixed* belay device or *fixed* mainline device, I'm really referring to the location of the device. In the case of *fixed*, the device is always rigged at the anchor and is typically controlled by someone independent of the load. When a device is in the *traveling* position it is typically attached to, and controlled by a person on rappel and it is indeed traveling up and/or down with that person. A dynamic anchor system is usually referring to the mainline and it is engineered to have adjustability, usually through the use of a mini-pulley system interfaced between the anchor and the device. You will see more of this example in the section on Dynamic Anchor Lowering Systems (DALS).

Belaying with the Petzl I'D (Fixed Position)

The Petzl I'D provides an excellent option for system belays, especially for industrial applications. The I'D truly passes all fail safe testing criteria. Rig the I'D in accordance to the Petzl User Manual. Manage the slack by pulling the rope connected to the load back towards the ID *(See Non-loaded Position below)*.

Petzl shows in their instructions that one hand should always hold the component of rope opposite the component of rope connected to the load. Following this technique of Petzl there is a tendency for two conditions to happen; the belayer can potentially introduce too much slack into longer systems, or the Petzl I'D simply locks up and the need to release tension with the handle is required.

During the belaying of raising systems; simply pull the standing end of the rope through the I'D with one hand, and with the other hand introduce the component of rope from the load side into the I'D. During all *non-loaded* belay applications, the handle stays in the neutral position. When leaving the belay station, rotate the handle to the locked position.

Loaded Position
(Mirrored System)

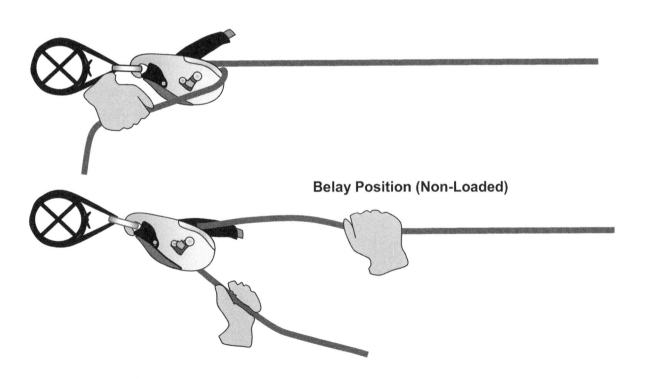

Belay Position (Non-Loaded)

Petzl ASAP Belay (Traveling Position)

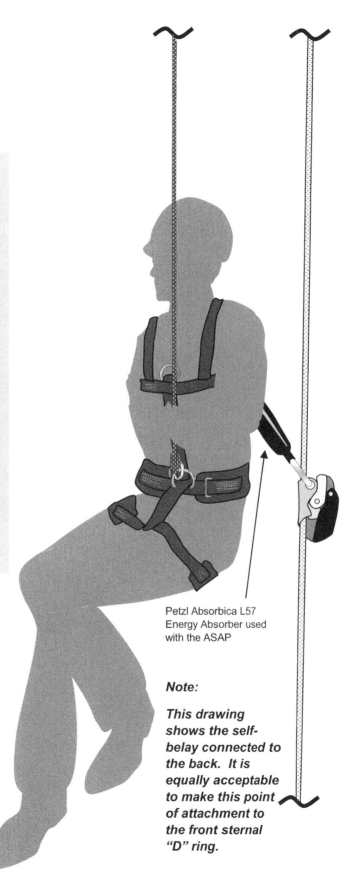

Note on the ASAP

The ASAP is easily adapted as a belay device for any vertical rescue. This is particularly useful when only one rescuer is performing a rescue from a crane.

The ASAP is connected to the victim's dorsal "D" ring and follows a fixed belay rope to the ground while the rescuer lowers the victim to the ground with the Petzl ID controlling the mainline.

Petzl Absorbica L57 Energy Absorber used with the ASAP

Note:

This drawing shows the self-belay connected to the back. It is equally acceptable to make this point of attachment to the front sternal "D" ring.

Rigging Petzl ASAP from a Fixed Anchor Point

The ASAP is extremely easy to use as a belay line/fall protection system that is attached to an anchor approved by the team leader. The fall arrest (Belay) rope is simply allowed to run through the ASAP as the load is lowered via the primary rope system. *Care must be taken to eliminate any buildup of slack in the belay rope between the ASAP and the load.*

This drawing is a manufacturer's approved belay method for a single person load. When belaying a two-person load with the ASAP rig the Petzl L57 Energy absorber between the anchor connection and the ASAP.

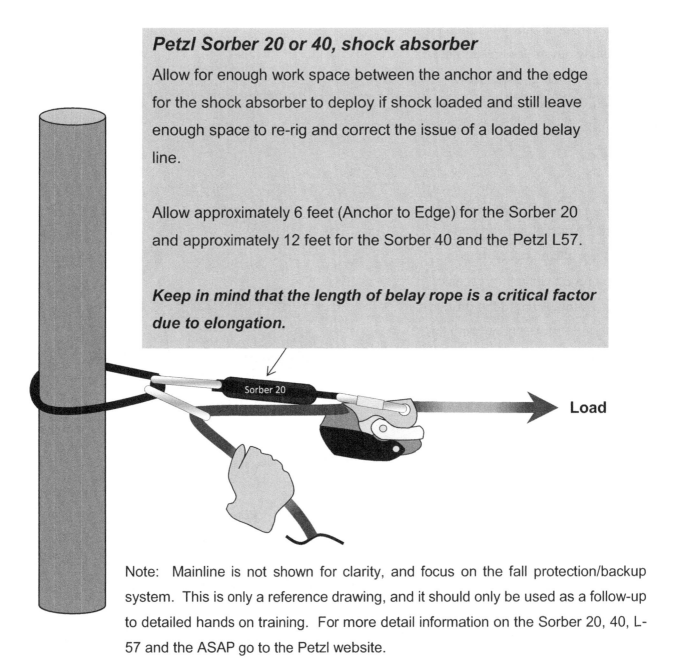

Petzl Sorber 20 or 40, shock absorber

Allow for enough work space between the anchor and the edge for the shock absorber to deploy if shock loaded and still leave enough space to re-rig and correct the issue of a loaded belay line.

Allow approximately 6 feet (Anchor to Edge) for the Sorber 20 and approximately 12 feet for the Sorber 40 and the Petzl L57.

Keep in mind that the length of belay rope is a critical factor due to elongation.

Note: Mainline is not shown for clarity, and focus on the fall protection/backup system. This is only a reference drawing, and it should only be used as a follow-up to detailed hands on training. For more detail information on the Sorber 20, 40, L-57 and the ASAP go to the Petzl website.

Petzl ASAP from a Fixed Anchor Point Continued...

The drawing below illustrates the Petzl ASAP rigged at an anchor during a raising process. By extending a directional pulley from the anchor and immediately behind the ASAP the operator can easily "up rope" the belay line and simultaneously control any possibility of slack in the Absorbica shock absorber and belay system.

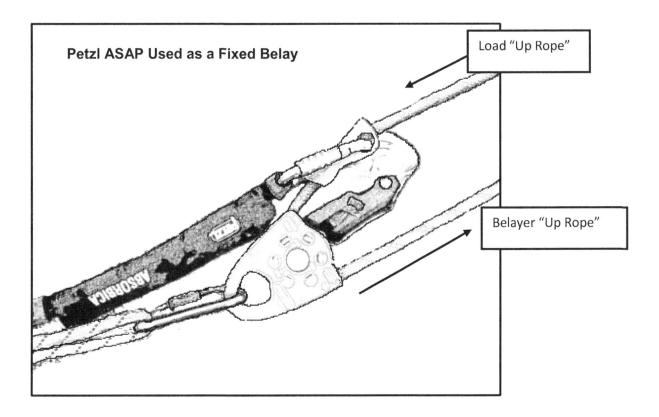

The Integration of the Mainline with Standards Compliancy

When building a mainline system, consider the possibility of the need to convert from a lowering system to a raising system. There are numerous hidden factors that have caught many teams by surprise. Life becomes much easier and safer by predicting these factors and pre-planning the Mainline when the time comes to convert to the raising system.

Typically, lowering systems are safer than raising systems because we are cooperating with gravity and friction. The moment we go to a raising system gravity and friction becomes our prime adversaries. In terms of rigging, we must pay close attention to the friction coefficient of our rope system and the surface between the anchor system and the rescue package. Yes, friction is working in our favor during the lowering process. When we are only going down the surface friction isn't that big of a deal (although we still keep a sharp eye out for rope abrasion and damage). However, when it is known that a raising system is going to be employed, we must mitigate rope contact with the surface before the lowering system is put into action. This is best accomplished by the use of a pulley rigged to a high directional anchor system.

The Theoretical Load Weight (TLW) is the weight of the load during a static state; the Practical Load Weight (PLW) is the actual weight of the load plus the effects of the friction coefficient. Unfortunately, this fact is often overlooked by many teams. During a lowering with approximately 20 feet of rope contact with a rock surface, the PLW of a 450-pound two-person load may be only 150 pounds. During a raise with the same 20 feet of rope drag, the PLW will skyrocket to about 1100 pounds!

What does this mean to our anchor selection? With the use of a high directional, the unwanted friction is all but eliminated. Without the use of a high directional, our anchor system is very susceptible to this hidden weight and possibly prone to failure. Control of all the many aspects of friction during a rope rescue operation is a must.

The Petzl ID: Using the Belay Line for Loaded Change Overs
(Replacing the mainline ID with a PMP and Ratchet Prusik)[vi]

Using the belay ID to facilitate a loaded change over to a hauling system and totally taking the mainline ID from the system is completely acceptable providing the mainline and belay line are within a couple of feet of each other. Transferring the weight of the load between the two different lines will have a cause and effect of the edge management. The best practice is to a have secure/bombproof high directional belay pulley and mainline pulley at the edge.

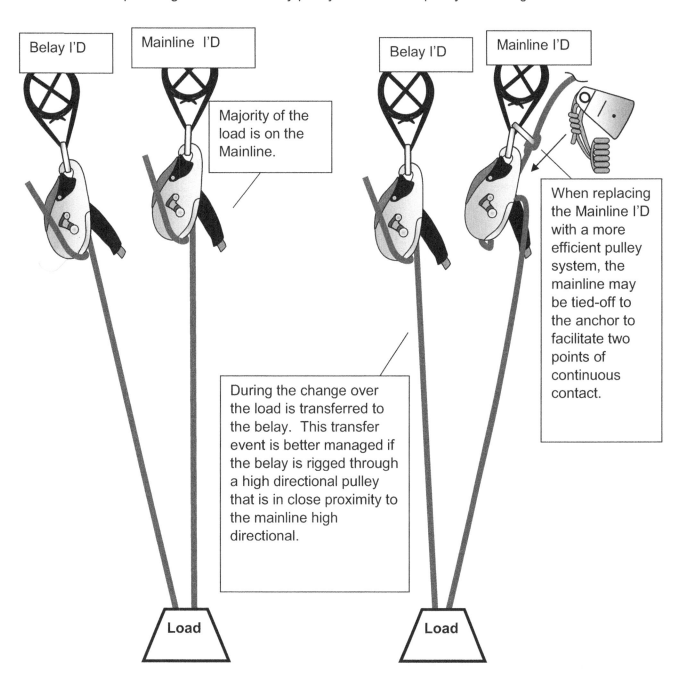

Pre-plan the Working Line

All too often, teams rig their haul system with the progress capture device (the ratchet) at a directional anchor located in front of the mechanical advantage system. This ratchet position is most often due to the lack of pre-planning the layout of the working/haul line system.

Usually the rigger will build the braking system for lowering at the anchor most in line with the fall line. Typically, this anchor is too close to the edge and offers a very small throw for the soon to become haul system. To overcome this problem, the team will then look for another anchor that will provide a longer throw and hauling field beyond, or to the side of the first anchor.

One problem leads to another. The working line, now in need of a hot change-over, (going from a lowering to a raising under tension) has only one place the brake system (lowering) can be replaced with a ratchet (raising). This is at the original anchor, the one closest to the edge, the one that is now a forward directional for the haul system.

There are some inherent problems with a ratchet that is in front of the MA. During the re-set phase of the haul, the rope behind the haul rope grab device is always slack, making for sloppy re-sets, but even more problematic, is the ebb and flow, back and forth movement of the directional anchor that occurs between re-sets and even at every tug of the rope. At best, this type of inefficient system mandates a back-tie that opposes the haul team.

As a result of this ebb and flow movement, the continual change in the force vector of the directional anchor gives us great concern to the integrity of the anchor. Keep in mind when looking at the drawings below, the static weight of the load at the directional anchor (non-moving, with equal tension on both sides of the directional pulley) is approximately 141% greater after the conversion to a raising system than it was during the lowering. The anchor stress will always be substantially greater during a haul than during a lowering. When choosing an anchor for a lowering system, we must build it strong enough to withstand the forces generated by the raising system that we will be going to later.

What is the friction profile of the edge? Are we making a 90-degree turn over sandstone or granite, or are we utilizing a high directional? During a raise, a 90-degree turn over a rock surface will add over 3 times the weight of the load at the edge. Using the force vector formula on page 114, one can quickly see the potential for a catastrophic failure of an underestimated directional anchor. The problem is magnified when the ratchet is put at the forward position. This constant change of low tension to high tension and back again is what has been the downfall of many anchors.

The solution to this problem is very simple: Pre-plan the best location for the future haul system and ratchet and put the braking device for the lowering at that position from the start.

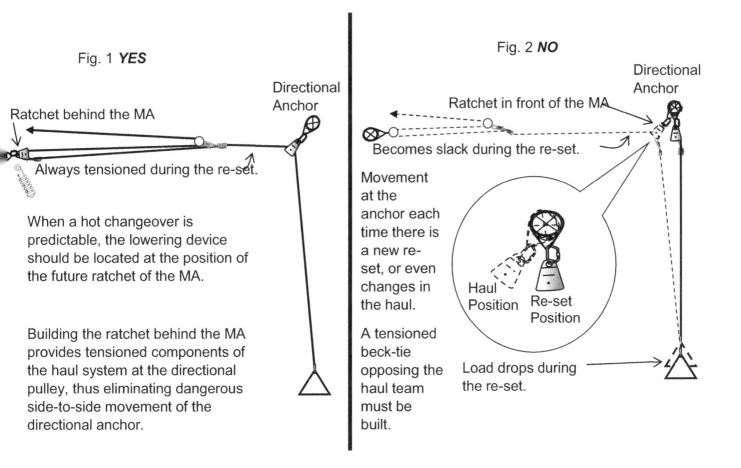

Dynamic Directionals (controlled anchor dynamics)[vii]

Dynamic Directional Anchors are adjustable pulleys/anchors. Being able to have a stable anchor and simultaneously move that anchor is only allowed when doing so under an extremely controlled and calculated manner. Many times, the interface of a simple 5:1 between a stable anchor and the directional pulley works well for smaller gaps. Larger gaps may require rigging that provides a somewhat larger amount of horsepower; at least a 6:1 or 9:1 compound system.

For short deviations, minor dynamic directional anchors may not require a belay for the point of horizontal influence; however, the belay option may be put into use based on the decision that the dynamic directional is indeed a critical safety element of the overall operation. The key question you must ask is, if the dynamic directional were to fail, would the pendulum effect of mainline cause serious injury to the rescue load?

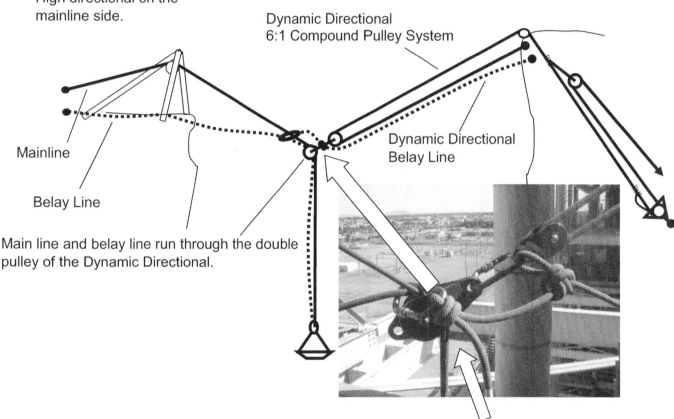

Dynamic Directional Anchor
High directional on the mainline side.

Low or high directional on the deflected offset side should be relatively parallel to the high directional on the mainline.

Dynamic Directional 6:1 Compound Pulley System

Mainline

Belay Line

Dynamic Directional Belay Line

Main line and belay line run through the double pulley of the Dynamic Directional.

The Dynamic Directional belay is tied in to the pulley carabiner with a "butterfly". A one-foot tail from the butterfly goes to a steel carabiner that encompasses the main line and belay line just above the double pulley.

Controlled Release Anchor Systems (C.R.A.S)

The concept of a Controlled Release Anchor System (CRSA) has been around since the advent of sailing. This is no more than tying off the anchor end of a descent line through a friction device (Petzl I'D, MPD, brake rack, munter hitch, etc.). Additionally, there must be enough stored rope behind the friction device to allow for the continuation of movement (usually lowering) once the backup tied-off friction device has been untied. This tool/rigging concept can safely and expediently rescue an incapacitated vertical worker/victim without having a rescuer go vertical to perform a pick-off. This is an invaluable rigging option for planned rope access events and standby rescue.

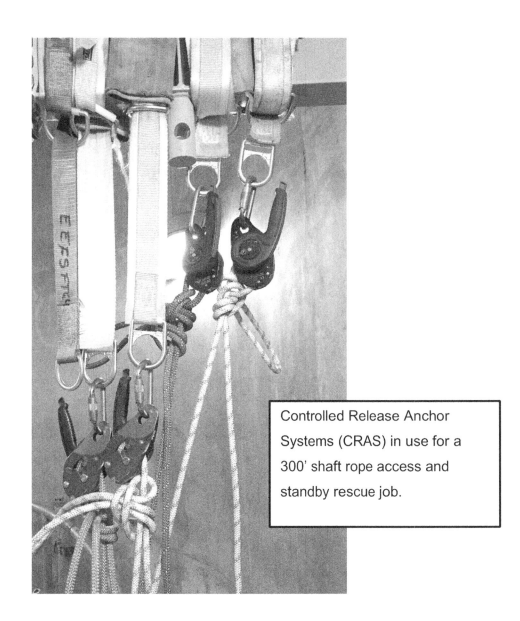

Controlled Release Anchor Systems (CRAS) in use for a 300' shaft rope access and standby rescue job.

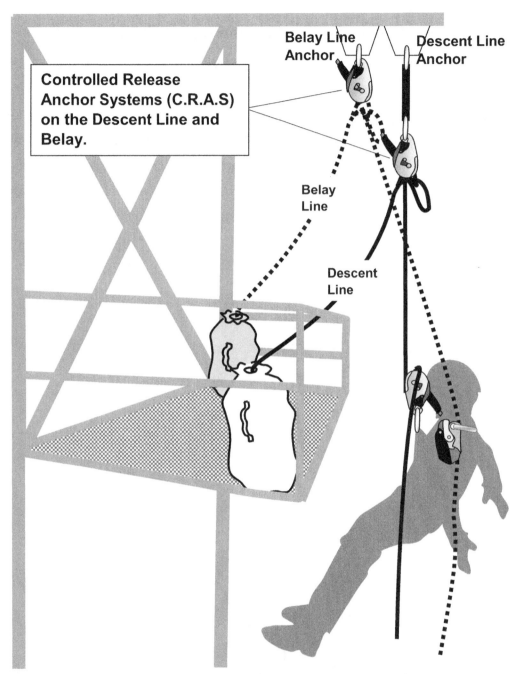

Controlled Release Anchor Systems (C.R.A.S) on the Descent Line and Belay.

In this example, the rappel line and the belay line are both rigged through CRAS anchors. The I'D handles are in the locked position. Best practice is to tie-off the CRAS devices with two half hitches during non-use. If the worker is unable continue the decent, there is a possibility that both traveling devices (the I'D and the ASAP) are loaded and/or locked off requiring use of both CRAS anchors. There are a number of descent devices that would work in this emergency release position, including a Munter Hitch dogged off with two Half Hitches.

Dynamic Anchor Lowering System (D.A.L.S.)

A prime directive of rigging is that anchors should never be subject to arbitrary or accidental movement. This is not to say that anchors must never move. In fact, purposeful and highly controlled movement of anchors is not only allowable, it may be absolutely required to complete a specific rigging task. The Dynamic Anchor Lowering System (DALS) is a rigging methodology designed to allow highly controlled anchor movement. Very simply, the DALS is nothing more than some form of inline pulley system interfaced between the fixed anchor and the descent device. Most often we use a mini-haul system as the inline pulley interface. This allows short, controlled movement, up or down, for the purpose of placing the descent device (and load) where we need it to be.

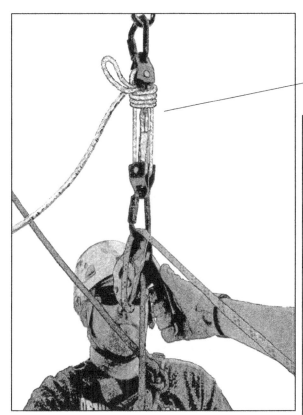

Dynamic Anchor Lowering System (D.A.L.S.)

Dynamic Anchor Lowering System (D.A.L.S.)

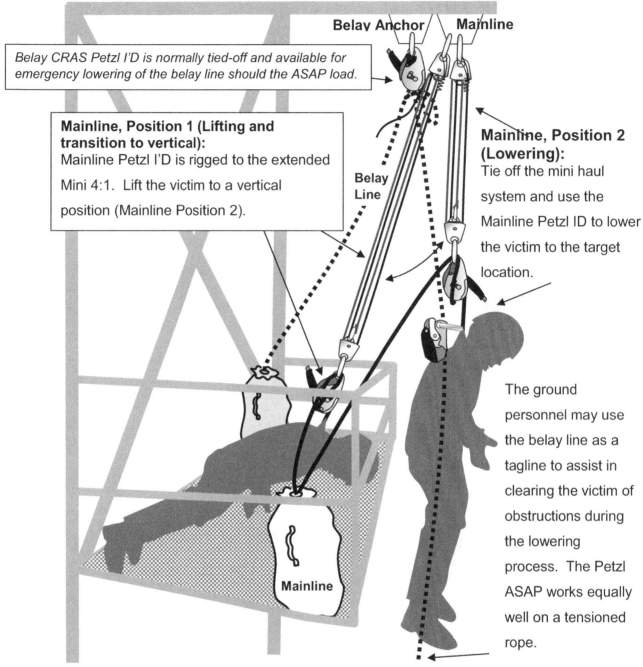

Belay CRAS Petzl I'D is normally tied-off and available for emergency lowering of the belay line should the ASAP load.

Mainline, Position 1 (Lifting and transition to vertical):
Mainline Petzl I'D is rigged to the extended Mini 4:1. Lift the victim to a vertical position (Mainline Position 2).

Mainline, Position 2 (Lowering):
Tie off the mini haul system and use the Mainline Petzl ID to lower the victim to the target location.

The ground personnel may use the belay line as a tagline to assist in clearing the victim of obstructions during the lowering process. The Petzl ASAP works equally well on a tensioned rope.

The belay shown in the diagram above is an auto belay using the Petzl ASAP. This system works well with limited manpower. In this example the ASAP belay is attached to the victim during the lift but just prior to putting the victim in a vertical exposure.

Note:
The belay line is tied off through a *Petzl I'D connected to the belay anchor*. The ID handle is in the locked position. In the event of the ASAP engaging (mainline failure or accidental loading), *This ID located at the belay anchor* can be used to complete the lowering of the victim with the belay line. There must be enough belay line in the belay bag to complete this function. There are a number of descent devices that would work in this emergency release position, including a Munter Hitch dogged off with two Half Hitches.

Useful Hauling System Schematics

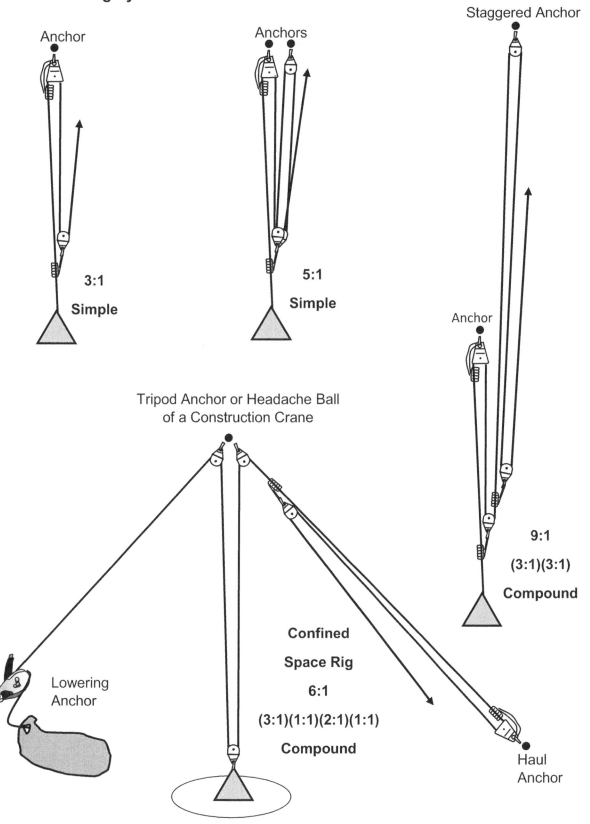

Personal Vertical Mobility

Descending, Ascending, and Horizontal Movement

Rappelling is a controlled descent down a fixed line. This is a skill that is generally taught to most fire/rescue personnel. However, many time this is also where the training stops. Make no mistake about it. The world of rope access is here to stay. Organizations such as ARAA, SPRAT and IRATA offer excellent instruction in rope access techniques. I would highly recommend these organizations to anyone involved in technical rescue for further direction in rope access skills. Where I see the most glaring deficiency in professional rescue is a lack of true vertical mobility. Along with the skill sets, is a full understanding of the current evolution of the equipment as it pertains to OSHA compliancy and modern rescue.

In this section called Vertical Mobility I am depicting a few rope access skills that I personally feel all rope rescue and confined space rescue technicians should be able to perform.

There are several skills necessary to rappel safely and effectively, including proper technique, understanding belay systems, and knowledge of anchor systems. As opposed to recreational or military rappelling, rope access/rescue rappelling is done in a slow and controlled manner. Rapid, bouncing rappels are a very unprofessional approach in reaching the victim. This kind of attitude can contribute to loss of control, rope damage, and potential system wide failure.

Always check your rigging, and have another team member double check your rigging, carabiners should be in the down, locked position. Make sure the helmet strap is secure, and gloves are on prior to beginning.

When rappelling, never take your brake hand off of the rope, unless the descent device is properly lock and/or tie-off. Make sure to take appropriate ascending devices with you in the event self-rescue becomes necessary.

Rescue and rope access operations should employ a separate belay line.

Selecting an anchor to rappel from is every bit as important as anchor selection for the system. Simply because the rappel rope is supporting a single person load doesn't lessen the fact that there is still at least one human life on rope, don't lose sight of this for the sake of speed.

The use of high directionals, either natural, structural, or artificial, is highly recommended whenever possible. The higher above the waistline the rappel rope is anchored the easier it will be to negotiate the edge.

Rappel Signals

Rappeller	**Belayer**
"Belay On?" (Is belayer ready?)	"On Belay." (Belayer is ready.)
"On Rappel?" (Rappeller is ready.)	"Rappel On."
"Slack." (Need slack in belay line.)	"Slack"
"Up Rope."	"Up Rope" (Belayer takes up slack.)
"Off Rope." (Rappeller finished and off)	

Signals anyone can make:
"Rock!"   (A rock is falling overhead.)
"Stop!"   (Cease all operations.)

OTHER CONSIDERATIONS

- Always address edge protection.
- Don't rush.
- The simplest way is often the most effective.
- Wear protective clothing when appropriate.
- Minimize the number of personnel near the edge.
- Use knives with extreme caution; rescue scissors are a better option.

You have a right to question authority. Make sure you feel comfortable with a given situation

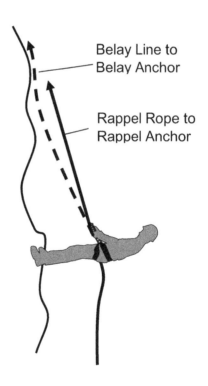

Correct rappel posture is typically:

- Feet placement about the same width as the rescuer's shoulders, wider if the terrain type dictates the need.

- With the body at a 90-degree angle to the surface being rappelled.

The rescuer should employ a separate belay rope. The rescuer's end of the belay should be tied to a dedicated point of attachment separate from the rappel line. Preferably the rescuer end of the belay line should be tied in such a way that the connecting knot captures the waist harness and the chest harness.

Belay Line to Belay Anchor

Rappel Rope to Rappel Anchor

Converting from Descent to Ascent and Vice Versa

Ascending Rope with the RAD System
(Rapid Ascend and Descend)

Rope may be ascended by using your hand ascender/foot loop and the Petzl I'D. As with all aspects of rope access, the user must be on a separate belay line (Shown in the drawing is the Petzl ASAP).

The RAD systems is a simple process of rigging a pulley on the top attachment hole of the hand ascender and running the non-loaded leg of the rappel rope up and through the pulley. This will give the user a 3:1 mechanical advantage. Combining the foot loop which is attached to the bottom of the hand ascender will allow for easy step and pull action for ascending the rope.

For a faster response, omit the 3:1 and simply pull slack through the I'D during the step-up move. Although this is quicker, it does require more effort and timing.

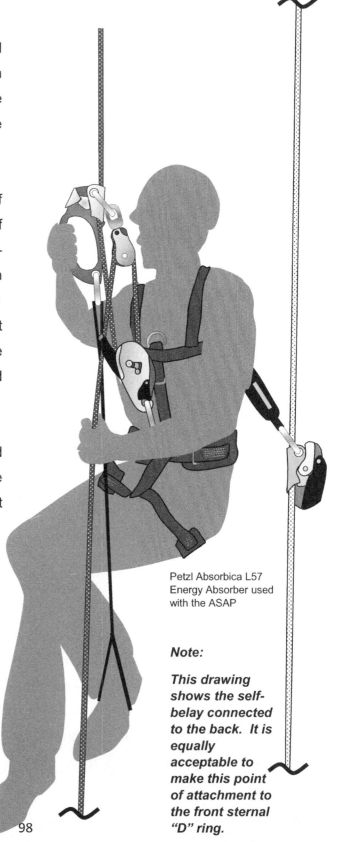

Petzl Absorbica L57 Energy Absorber used with the ASAP

Note:

This drawing shows the self-belay connected to the back. It is equally acceptable to make this point of attachment to the front sternal "D" ring.

Any rescue (especially in vertical confined space locations) must be able to convert from a descending position to an ascend while still on rope. There are a multitude of descending and ascending devices that can safely be used. What I'm showing here is my personal preference of using the Petzl I'D in combination with a hand ascender and appropriate foot-loop. Please keep in mind that these techniques require the help of a qualified instructor if you have never tried this activity before. Attempting to learn this activity simply from reading a book in not recommended.

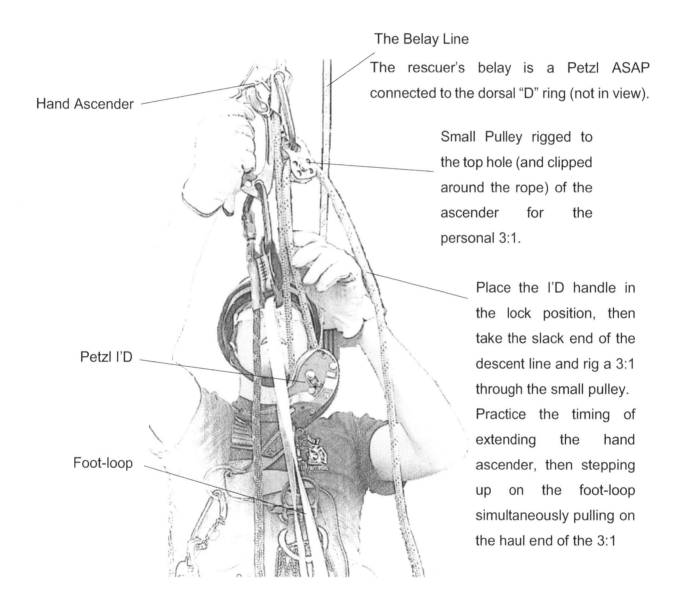

Hand Ascender

Petzl I'D

Foot-loop

The Belay Line

The rescuer's belay is a Petzl ASAP connected to the dorsal "D" ring (not in view).

Small Pulley rigged to the top hole (and clipped around the rope) of the ascender for the personal 3:1.

Place the I'D handle in the lock position, then take the slack end of the descent line and rig a 3:1 through the small pulley. Practice the timing of extending the hand ascender, then stepping up on the foot-loop simultaneously pulling on the haul end of the 3:1

Rope to Rope Transfer

A rope-to-rope traverse is a form of horizontal movement that requires the use of two rope systems (two mainlines and two belay lines). A common technique (as shown in the picture below) is to use simply two ropes (main and belay) drooped between anchors at the beginning point and the ending point. The rescuer/attendant/worker is equipped with two sets of descent/ascent systems. While descending on one side, slack is taken up and an ascending system is employed to the opposite side. This movement of descending one side and ascending to the other side will allow for very controlled, single operator horizontal movement.

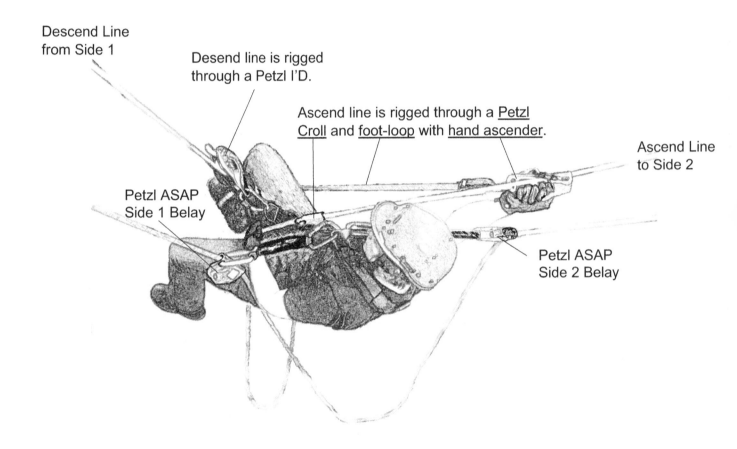

Towers and Vertical Confined Space Structures
Controlled Release Anchor System (C.R.A.S.)
Sloping Highline/Skate-Block

The Controlled Release Anchor System (C.R.A.S.) consist of an emergency descent control device (22kNMBS; MPD, or I'D w/shock absorber) plus an adequate amount of topside rope to lower the worker who as loaded and jammed on the high-tension belay device. During this event, the ground crew will maintain the proper amount of tension to clear potential obstacles by utilizing the bottom 3:1 pulley system. The topside will control the lowering of the stuck/injured worker with the CRAS.

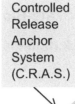

Controlled Release Anchor System (C.R.A.S.)

High tension capable belay device like the ASAP.

Highline is controlled by a 3:1 pulley system on the ground.

Haul line (Skate-block), is controlled by a capstan or pulley system on the ground.

Sloping Highline with Bottom Haul

- In this example of an oil-refinery refracting tower, this rope access option is controlled primarily by the ground team.
- The haul line (rigged as a skate-block) is controlled on the ground by a capstan wench. The highline tensioning system is also controlled on the ground by a 3:1 pulley system.
- The trolley system is rigged with tandem pulleys running in series between the highline pulley and the skate block pulley.
- A high-tension compliant belay device is rigged on the "up" side of the highline trolley and connected between the highline and the victim/worker. This belay device must be capable of moving freely up or down the tensioned highline, and yet, auto lock (without damaging the highline) in the event of a failure of the skate-block. Currently, the only device I feel comfortable with in this capacity is the Petzl ASAP.

Sloping Highline/Skate-Block Carriage Schematic continued

Sloping Highline/Skate-Block Continued

Sloping-Skate Block Highline Continued

Petzl ASAP rigged to the highline and in front of the carriage system.

Sloping Highline

Petzl Tandem Pulley connect to e the Tandem pulley on the Skate-Block via a carabiner.

ASAP/L57 rigged to the Skate-Block yoke.

Skate-Block to haul system or capstan winch.

There are a number of ways to rig the ASAP to facilitate two points of contact. In this version, the victim's belay is a fall arrest system attached to a 27kN Dyneema sling. The Dyneema sling is capturing all points at the yoke.

Primary attachment for the rescuer is a mini-haul system.

Highline Rigging Suggestions

Mitigating Shock Loads with I'D and the Yates Shorty in Highline Applications

Yates *Shorty* Shock Absorber

These configurations are somewhat different from the traditional brake-rack/tandem prusik control line rig. Tests have shown the Petzl I'D to work very well for control line operations. Combined with a single Yate's Shorty and a basket hitch (typically a doubled 8mm prusik loop) the I'D will provide the needed shock absorption in the event of a trackline failure.

Note on Highline Failures and Shock Absorption:
Recent class studies that I have been involved in suggest that the shock force produced during a highline failure and resulting in the capture of the load by the control lines is not a single location event. It is believed that a wave emits from the source (usually the carriage) and travels to each control anchor then back again, repeating shock waves until completely dissipated. This concept suggests that shock absorbers at the carriage and the anchors will help dissipate this wave.

Option 1: Basket Hitch; doubled long 8mm prusik; the load is on the "Shorty", during a trackline failure the "Shorty" will deploy stitches and gently transfer the load to the basket hitch. The rating of the 8mm basket hitch configuration is considered a high strength anchor ≥ 36kN.

Option 2: Instead of the Basket Hitch, we may choose to simply employ two Shorties as shown below working in conjunction with an I'D.

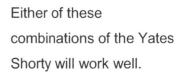

Either of these combinations of the Yates Shorty will work well.

Option 1 will deploy at 2 kN and safely load the basket hitch, whereas *Option 2* will deploy at 4kN and suffice as the sole anchor interface. *Option 1* works well with added absorbers rigged into the carriage system, while *Option 2* arguably eliminates the need for additional shock absorbers at the carriage.

Why Highlines?

Whereas extensive highlines combined with elaborate reeving systems has limited use in rope rescue, a strong argument can be made for this type of rigging in the realm of rope access and work positioning. The key factors shown here are shock mitigation in the form of legitimate manufactured shock absorbers. The old technique of prusik bypasses should only be used as a last resort.

Reeving Systems:

Any number of reeving systems can be employed from the portable carriage anchor.

Maintaining a reliable belay system is mandatory for any rope access event. The old technique of opposing prusiks for a reeve system is highly questionable given the propensity of failure of prusik belays on tensioned rope…the jury is still in deliberation on the use of prusiks for reeve system belays. Employing proven belay devices like the Petzl ASAP is currently the best practice.

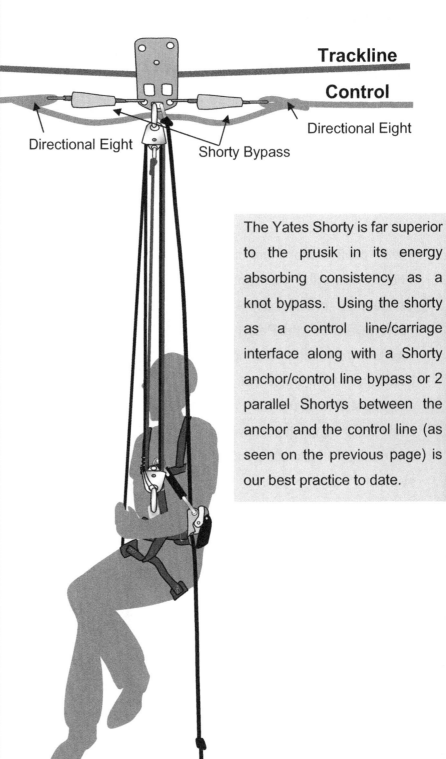

Trackline
Control
Directional Eight
Directional Eight
Shorty Bypass

The Yates Shorty is far superior to the prusik in its energy absorbing consistency as a knot bypass. Using the shorty as a control line/carriage interface along with a Shorty anchor/control line bypass or 2 parallel Shortys between the anchor and the control line (as seen on the previous page) is our best practice to date.

A Practitioner's Study Volume 2:
Insights Into Confined Space Rescue
© 2018, Rhodes

Single Carriage/English Reeve, using Opposing ASAP Reeve Belay

English reeves and Norwegian reeves are extremely useful for deeper drops.

Reeving Systems:

Any number of reeving systems can be employed from the portable carriage anchor.

As stated earlier, maintaining a reliable belay system is mandatory for any rope access event. I've now replaced the old technique of the opposing prusik belay for a reeve system with opposing ASAPS. The ASAPs have proven themselves time and again as a reliable fall arrest component when working in conjunction with tensioned rope. In addition, the ASAPs are substantially easier to tend than opposing prusiks for this application.

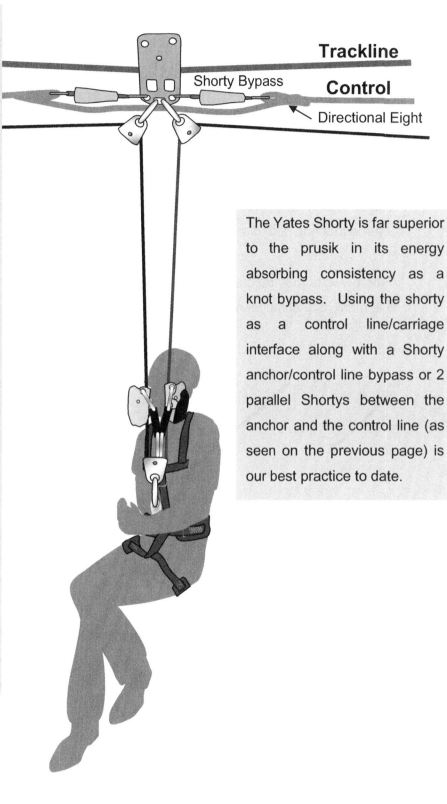

The Yates Shorty is far superior to the prusik in its energy absorbing consistency as a knot bypass. Using the shorty as a control line/carriage interface along with a Shorty anchor/control line bypass or 2 parallel Shortys between the anchor and the control line (as seen on the previous page) is our best practice to date.

Appendix 1: Applied Rigging Physics[viii]

Resultants:

Force Vectors[ix]

To have a better understanding on how force acts upon any anchor at least some aspects of trigonometry and vector physics is desirable. The knowledge of angles, components, and resultants is synonymous to quality rope rigging. To study vectors is to study the physical qualities of force that has both direction and magnitude.

A force vector may be graphed or represented as a simple arrow, also more commonly referred to in math as a component. This component will always indicate the direction of the force.

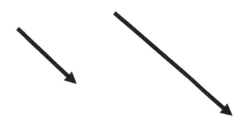

When we compare the length of one force vector component to the length of another force vector component, we not only have the direction of each vector, but we now can compare their magnitude relative to each other.

Therefore, the component that is the longest has a greater magnitude. In fact, simply by comparing the two components we could deduce that the second component (above) is about 2 times more powerful or stronger than the first.

The force of any resultant/ vector acting upon any two components of an angle can be realized by drawing a parallelogram that matches the components and is bisected by the vector component. *Within the boundaries of the parallelogram* we can simply measure each of the three components (C1, C2, and R) and based on the known magnitude of the resultant (R) we can then assign a value to C1 and C2.

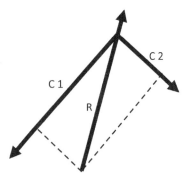

When a rope runs through a pulley to create an angle, the pulley equalizes the components of that angle and renders them equal. The resultant (in this case, the pulley) will always seek the location halfway between the two rope components.

The center of any tensioned pulley will always point to the exact location and direction of the resultant force at work on the associated anchor.[x]

The use of the parallelogram still works well in determining the resultant force, its direction and magnitude. Once again, the resultant of any pulley will find the middle point between the legs of rope going in and coming out of the pulley.

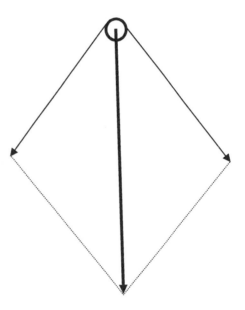

The resultant of an equalized pulley is the absolute indicator of where the force of that pulley is directed.

Study the two right angle rope systems below; both have two anchors and both support a 100kg load. What percentage of the load is each anchor receiving?

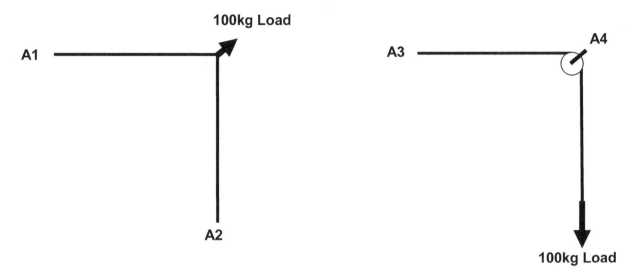

If you said A1 and A2 receive 71kg; A3 receives 100kg; and A4 receives 141kg you would be correct.

Let's look at these right angles again and apply our parallelogram/resultant analysis:

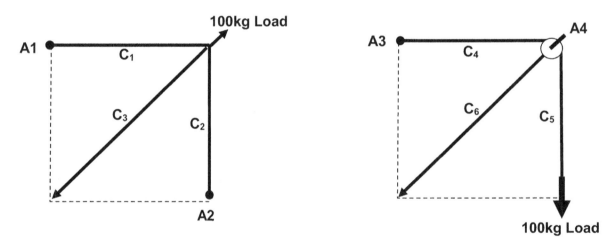

The 100kg load is our known value, whatever component the load is in line with represents 100% of that load; the remaining two components may now be assigned a value simply by comparing their length. C_3 = 100%, therefore C_1 and C_2 are 71% of C_3. C_5 = 100%, therefore C_4 = 100% of C_5 and C_6 = 141% of C_5.

Although using parallelograms as mentioned above to determine the resultant of any given angle is a good rule of thumb method, ultimately, for field application we must commit to rote memory the recognition of angles as they apply to either, 1) multipoint anchor systems, or 2) directional pulley anchors.

Force Vector Formula for Directional Pulley Anchors

% of Load on Pulley Anchor = $\cos\{<(0.5)\}(2)$

< = Pulley Vector Angle

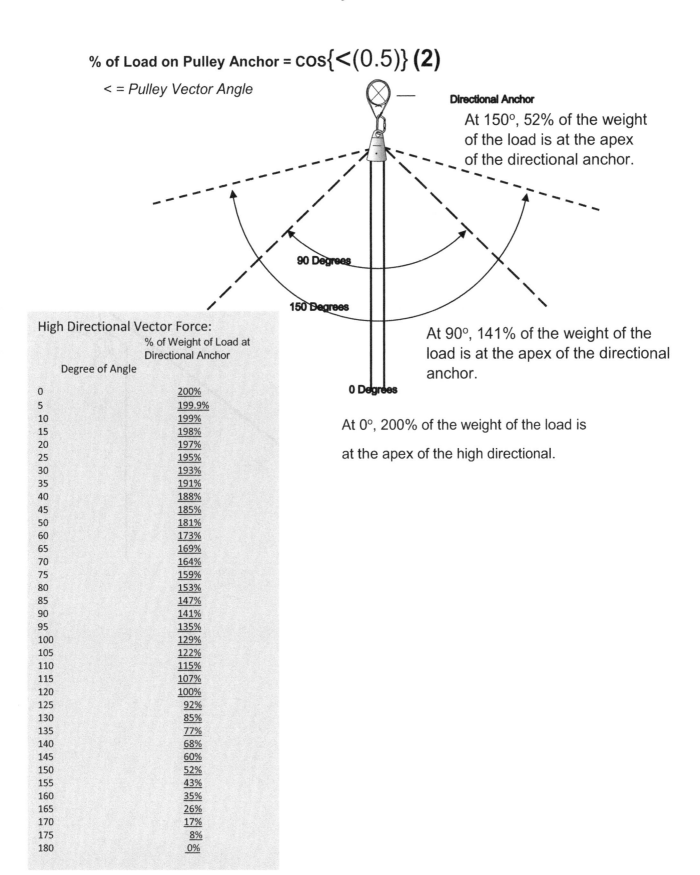

Directional Anchor

At 150°, 52% of the weight of the load is at the apex of the directional anchor.

At 90°, 141% of the weight of the load is at the apex of the directional anchor.

At 0°, 200% of the weight of the load is at the apex of the high directional.

High Directional Vector Force:

Degree of Angle	% of Weight of Load at Directional Anchor
0	200%
5	199.9%
10	199%
15	198%
20	197%
25	195%
30	193%
35	191%
40	188%
45	185%
50	181%
60	173%
65	169%
70	164%
75	159%
80	153%
85	147%
90	141%
95	135%
100	129%
105	122%
110	115%
115	107%
120	100%
125	92%
130	85%
135	77%
140	68%
145	60%
150	52%
155	43%
160	35%
165	26%
170	17%
175	8%
180	0%

Force Vector Formula for Multipoint Anchors

$$T = \frac{(L)(.5)}{\cos \phi}$$

By using this basic trigonometry function we are able to look at ½ of the entire system. Doing so, we can derive the amount of tension at one anchor by creating a right angle between the resultant component of the load and one leg of the system.

The tension of one leg of the vector angle is realized by dividing ½ the load by cos ϕ (the ratio of the sag over one leg of the vector angle; adjacent/hypotenuse).

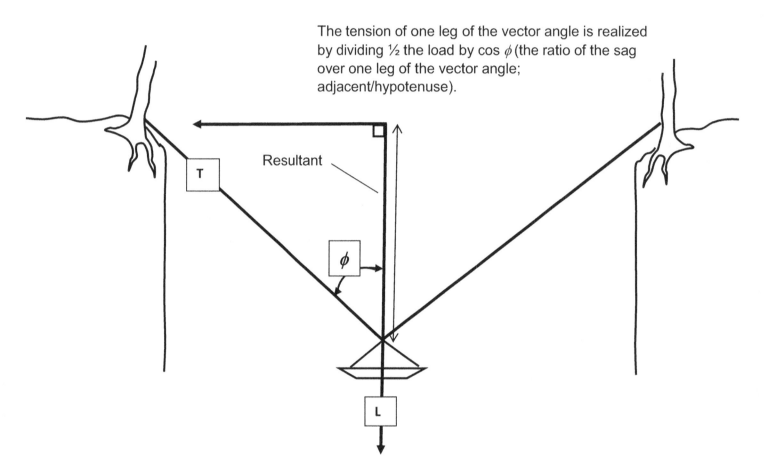

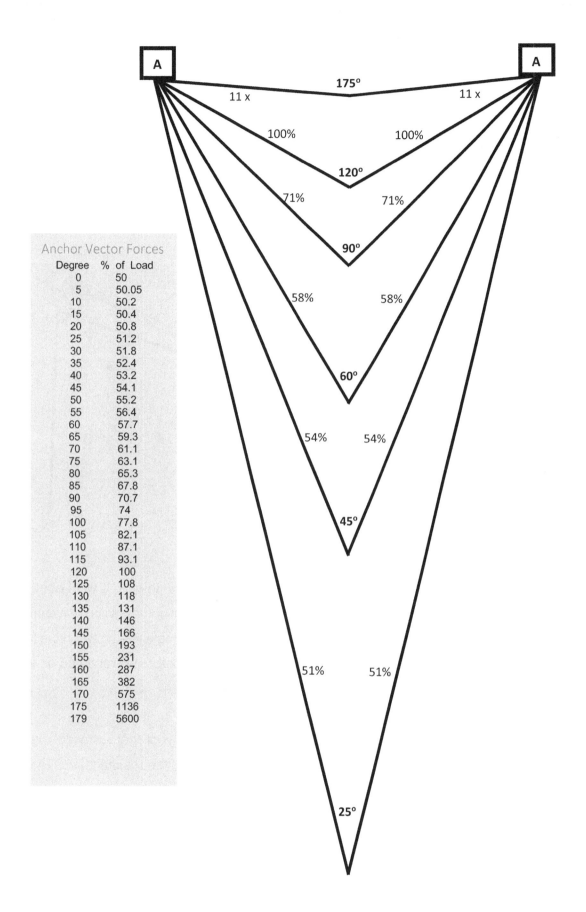

A Practitioner's Study Volume 2:
Insights Into Confined Space Rescue
© 2018, Rhodes

Tensile and Compression Force

Footprints – a prelude to understanding compression
What is meant by the *"footprint"* of a tripod? Most rescue techs understand this term when using a tripod...but what about other forms of anchors, especially elevated anchor systems?

The footprint is exactly what it says. The footprint you make in the sand is created by the compression of your body weight on your leg and down to your feet. Therefore, we can say the footprint represents compression. The same criterion applies to all artificial high directionals (AHDs) such as tripods, bi-pods, and mono-pods. The footprint defines the area of compression between the legs of these anchors.

Tri-pods

The resultant must stay within the triangle area "footprint" created by the legs.

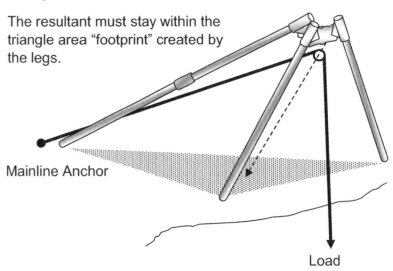

Mainline Anchor

Load

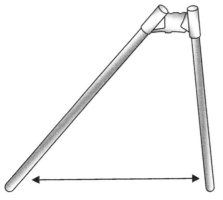

The footprint of an "A" Frame is a single line between the legs.

The tripod is a very visual triangle...but what about an "A" frame (bi-pod); the area of compression between the two legs is now limited to a single line between the legs. The gin pole's (mono-pod) footprint is rendered down to a single point

Stand up and take a look at your feet...why do you not fall over? The answer is that the resultant force of your body is perfectly focused on that invisible line that defines the area of compression between your feet (footprint). The moment that you lean your body backwards you focus your body weight (resultant force) backwards and you start to fall, thus the need for something to grab a hold of to prevent the fall (a back-tie). In a hypothetical perfect world of balance, we would be able to keep our high directional pulley focused right on that single line defining the footprint of an "A" frame and it would never tip over, or we could keep our gin pole from falling simply by focusing the high directional pulley straight down the pole on its single footprint.

Of course, we know this is virtually impossible. We will always have some movement due to elongation of the ropes in the back-ties, and inefficiencies of the pulleys. Therefore, the ability to rig quality back-ties and accurately engineer the resultant of the pulleys to maximize the compression of the legs is vital for advance use of AHDs.

In the application of rigging, we must address tension and compression at the same time. Most of us associate units of tension with the study of pulleys and mechanical advantage systems. While this is indeed a critical factor of pulley systems, it is important to remember that the same physics that characterize tension in the study of pulley systems is also applicable to every single act of rope rigging. The instant a single piece of rope is tied and loaded, units of tension become a factor.

Compressive and tensile forces are symbiotic. As with all forms of construction, (rope rigging included) one cannot exist without the other. Not only must harmony exist between tension and compression, there must be equal synchronization with all aspects of rigging physics. The bottom line revolves around the anchors. Will they hold, or won't they? What is the exact force vector being applied to the anchor? What is the resultant on the anchor? Is there an adequate amount of tension/compression at work to guarantee the integrity of the anchor?

Tension, Compression, Friction

Rigging is the use of tension and compression to either move something or to keep something in place. Whether we are moving or holding something, friction is always there, working for us or against us. This section on friction is a basic treatment of coefficients of friction with a specific focus on how it will multiply the weight of the actual load during a hauling.

It is common practice in rope rescue to use a friction device such as a Petzl I'D for the addition of friction during a lowering. When the mainline come in contact with the edge during a lowering it is as if an additional brake rack has been added. Aside from any rope wear and tear of continual edge contact, this edge friction is working in our favor.

Now let's convert our lowering to a raising system; the same edge contact that was working in our favor on the way down is now playing tug-of-war with the haul team! A matter of fact, a good rule-of-thumb measurement is about 3 times the weight of the load is really what the haul team has to overcome when the rope is being pulled over a rock ledge. This is arguably the single most important reason for the use of elevated anchor systems (the Vortex Multipod, or TerrAdpapter, natural or structural) over difficult edges.

Traditionally, we have always perform a Static System Safety Factor (SSSF) prior to the implementation of a rope rescue; we analyzed our rigging and made a judgment of the weakest link and whether or not it was within the parameters of our safety margin, usually a 10:1. The Dynamic System Safety Factor (DSSF) on the other hand, judges the rigging system during its operation, and predicts the weakest link during the greatest moment of system stress? This moment of greatest stress will always be during the transition between a static state to a state of hauling, or put into physical terms; the *transition from static friction to dynamic friction (sliding friction)*.

Friction Law

Friction is a force of resistance between two objects that tends to oppose any motion. Friction may be further defined as being either static friction (force that tends to counter motion of an object that is in a state of rest, and kinetic friction (force wanting to slow an object in motion).

Dynamic Friction

After the initial spike of needed force to move the object from a state of rest, the dynamic friction (sliding friction) is the force needed to sustain movement over the surface.

Appendix 2: Elevated Anchor Systems[xi]
Back-tie Schematics for Elevated Anchor Guying Systems

Most rope rescue personnel who experiment with all these variations of elevated anchors usually agree on one thing…. Sideways A Frame *(SA)* Frame is by far the safest, user-friendly, and resultant accommodating of the whole lot. Because of this, we feel compelled to talk a bit more about some additional rigging tips concerning the SA frame.

To the right; as seen in this photo of a challenging industrial enclosed space extrication, the SA frame can fit in extremely tight locations such as industrial catwalks. The rules still apply when choosing the guying anchors for the tension back-ties. When eyeing from one back-tie anchor to the other, this visual straight edge should bisect the middle of the plane created by the front and back legs of the SA frame.

Many times when the back-tie anchors don't quite line up, the SA frame may be rotated to make the plane of the legs accommodate the back-tie anchors.

Note the photo to the left. Although this is a Vortex Multi-pod system, this rigging example still applies to the TerrAdaptor.

This is a view looking up at the head of a SA Frame; this is a good example showing the tensioned guying system pulling opposite directions. Note that they are connected to the same location on the head; unwanted torque will arise if one back-tie is forward on the head and the opposite back-tie is rigged to the back end of the head. In addition, when more radical HD (High Directional) pulley resultants are predicted, the HD pulley should be rigged as close as possible to the same location on the head as the guying system.

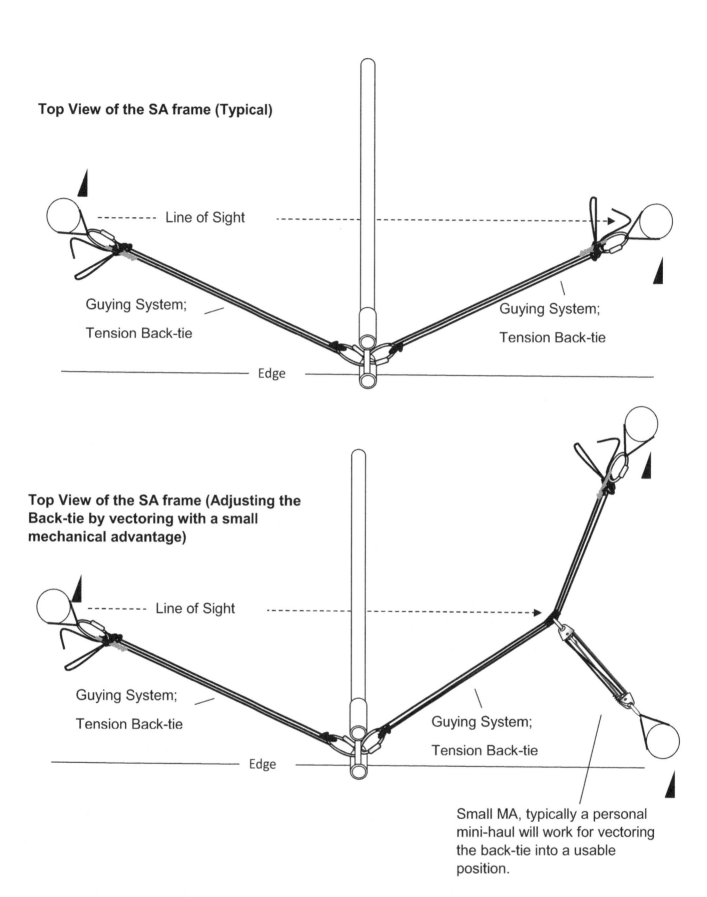

End Notes:

[i] These stages of learning have been frequently attributed to Abraham Maslow, however, it is generally thought that this theory was developed by Noel Burch during the 1970s while under the employment of Gordon Training International.

[ii] OSHA1910 Subpart H-Hazardous Materials, is a mandatory regulation in the United States. Per this Subpart, standard,1910;120 Appendix B; personal protective clothing (and equipment) is divided into four categories based on the degree of protection needed.
The following is a summary of the PPE requirements of this regulation for greater details of this standard go to www.osha.gov/laws-regs/regulations/standardnumber/1910/1910.120AppB ,

Level A, at a minimum, typically requires the following:
1. Positive pressure, full face-piece self-contained breathing apparatus (SCBA) (NIOSH approved).
2. Totally-encapsulating chemical-protective suit.
3. Gloves, outer, chemical-resistant.
4. Gloves, inner, chemical-resistant.
5. Boots, chemical-resistant, steel toe and shank.

Level B, at a minimum, typically requires the following:
1. Positive pressure, full-facepiece self-contained breathing apparatus (SCBA) (NIOSH approved).
2. Hooded chemical-resistant clothing.
3. Gloves, outer, chemical-resistant.
4. Gloves, inner, chemical-resistant.
5. Boots, chemical-resistant, steel toe and shank.

Level C, at a minimum, typically requires the following:
1. Full-face or half-mask, air purifying respirator, (NIOSH approved).
2. Gloves, outer, chemical-resistant.
3. Gloves, inner, chemical-resistant.
4. Boots, chemical-resistant, steel toe and shank.
5. Escape mask.
6. Face shield.

Level D, at a minimum, typically requires the following:
1. Coveralls.
2. Gloves
3. Boots/shoes, chemical-resistant steel toe and shank
4. Safety glasses or chemical splash goggles
5. Escape mask (if applicable).

[iii] Fix and Traveling Systems – Back in my days with Reed Thorne and RTR we often referred to a descent device and/or belay device that was attached at the anchor and typically controlled by an independent operator as being "Fixed". Of course, the same devices when used for rappelling was indeed traveling and therefor was classified as a traveling system. This classification has always made sense to me and like much of the rigging terminology I learned in those formative RTR days, I still use them today.

[iv] Taken from Rhodie's Guide to Rescue Knots, 3th Edition of Knots for the Rescue Service, © 2014, Rhodes

[v] See end note iii

[vi] The act of switching from a lowering system to a raising system, or vice versa, is a simple concept that often confuses many rope technicians. Simply put, the mainline must be captured

in front of the friction control device. With some descent control devices such as the MPD or the ID, this mainline capture is automatic, the rigger only needs to build the pulley system in front of the descent control. In the case of the ID, using it as the progress capture of an integrated pulley system is very inefficient and sometimes replacing the ID with a conventional prusik minding pulley may be needed.

[vii] I like to use the term Dynamic Directional to reflect any directional pulley that requires extremely controlled adjustability. This can be as simple as a mini-haul system used to adjust the height of the belay line at the edge, or something more grandiose as seen in this drawing. This particular example of rigging is also commonly known as a Deflection Offset. I first learned this rigging technique while working with Reed Thorne and Ropes That Rescue.

[viii] Appendix 1: Applied Rigging Physics – This information on rigging physics is taken in its entirety from my book; A Practitioner's Study About Rope Rescue Rigging. I included this as an appendix as a quick reference to other aspects of rigging discussed throughout the body of this book.

[ix] References:
College Physics Enhanced 7th ed. ©2006 Raymond A. Serway
    Chapter 3, Vectors and Two-Dimensional Motion

Schaum's A-Z Physics, © 1997, 2000, 2003, Michael Chapple
    Vector Addition
    Parallelogram Law

[x] It should be noted that this statement is correct most of the time. However, when the end of the rope (opposite the load end) is connected to the same anchor that the directional pulley is connected to, the primary force acting on the anchor is now represented by the leg of rope connected to the load. This is commonly seen when a capstan wench is mounted to the leg of a tripod. With the haul end of the rope connected directly to a leg, the resultant of the directional pulley attached to the top of the tripod does not indicate the forces at play on the tripod. Given this scenario, if the load does shift outside of the footprint, the tripod will tip over.

[xi] Appendix 2: Elevated Anchor Systems Back-tie Schematics - This information is taken in its entirety from my book; A Practitioner's Study About Rope Rescue Rigging. I included this as an appendix as a quick reference to other aspects of rigging discussed throughout the body of this book.

About the Author

Pat "Rhodie" Rhodes is a native of Phoenix Arizona. Pat's career in technical rescue spans over 40 years. In 2005 Pat retired from the Phoenix Fire Department after 28 plus years of service as a technical rescue lead instructor and a veteran firefighter. During his career with Phoenix he also served as a Rescue Specialist for FEMA Arizona Task Force 1, and was a member of the Technical Rescue Validation committee for IFSTA (International Fire Service Training Association). His specialties are in Rigging Physics, Rope Access, Rope Rescue, Confined Space Rescue, and Tower Rescue. Pat has consulted and/or instructed fire department and technical rescue teams internationally.
Contact Pat at: *rescuerig@gmail.com*

Made in the USA
Monee, IL
26 June 2023

37599134R00066